WILD AND OLD GARDEN ROSES

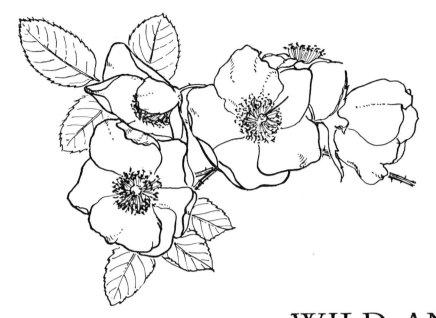

WILD AND
OLD GARDEN ROSES

With 31 color plates

GORDON EDWARDS

Line illustrations by Denys Baker

HAFNER PRESS
A Division of Macmillan Publishing Co., Inc.
New York

HAFNER PRESS
A Division of Macmillan Publishing Co., Inc.
866 Third Avenue, New York, N.Y. 10022

Library of Congress Cataloging in Publication Data
Edwards, Gordon, 1899–
    Wild and old garden roses.
    1. Roses—Varieties.   2. Rose Culture.
I. Title.
SB411.E289 1975   635.9'33'372   74-18490

'Indeed, he was a man keenly alive
to the beauty of all that was bygone'

An Old Scotch Gardener
Robert Louis Stevenson

DEDICATION

Gratitude is but a lame sentiment; thanks when they are expressed, are often more embarrassing than welcome; and yet I must set forth mine to Graham Stuart Thomas, VMH, horticulturist – Garden Consultant to The National Trust, for having by his writings introduced me – an ordinary gardener – to the wild and old garden roses or, as he has termed them, *The Old Shrub Roses*, and who, in this and more esoteric spheres, has done so much to keep alive and to encourage an increasing interest in the predecessors of our present-day roses. To me, who finds it so difficult to tell the little that I know, he stands essentially as a *genius loci*.

CONTENTS

LIST OF ILLUSTRATIONS

ACKNOWLEDGEMENTS

The dedication of this book, *ipso facto*, acknowledges my indebtedness to Graham Stuart Thomas for quotations from his definitive books on roses – *The Old Shrub Roses, Shrub Roses of Today* and *Climbing Roses Old and New*: to this I add my thanks to his publishers, J. M. Dent & Sons Ltd, as regards the two last and David Higham Associates as to the first.

My thanks are given to The Hamlyn Publishing Group for permission to quote from Edward A. Bunyard's *Old Garden Roses*, and similarly to Macmillan Publishing Co, Inc, for giving permission for the reprinting of extracts from Roy E. Shepherd's *History of the Rose*, copyrighted 1954 by that company.

Permission to quote from David McClintock's *Companion to Flowers* was kindly given by Ward Lock & Co and by Bell & Sons Ltd. And in the context of the latter I am very grateful to an old friend, Michael Varvill, CMG, lately a director, for piloting me through the shoals of copyright.

I thank too Constables for allowing quotations from *Lord M* by David Cecil.

The bibliography noted by these and other erudite writers on the subjects dealt with in this book is most extensive: for instance, Graham Thomas lists just on ninety and Shepherd almost precisely double that number. Naturally I do not pretend to have read this mass of literature – duplicated as sometimes it may be.

I am grateful to Nancy Steen of New Zealand and to her and my (*Roses for Enjoyment*) publishers there, A. H. & A. W. Reed of Wellington, for enabling me to consult her comprehensive *The Charm of Old Roses* – so adding to my own much more limited experience – and to make quotations therefrom.

I want also to record my admiration for all those botanists, scientists and writers who have made, what is to me such erudite, skilful and painstaking research into the *genus rosa*, especially in the identification, parentage and history of the varieties. They are – Dr C. C. Hurst, Gordon D. Rowley and, once again, Graham S. Thomas.

I wish to mention, specially – *The Rose Fancier's Manual* (1838) written, one hundred and thirty-six years ago, by a lady described on the title pages as 'Mrs Gore', but whose more specific identification was particularised by the initials 'C.F.G.' under the Preface.

This lady has recently been described, on two occasions, as a plagiarist, that is, according to the *O.E.D.* – 'one who takes and uses another person's thoughts, writings, inventions ... as one's own'. This and other charges against the lady are dealt with in this book. My own immediate point is, however, that in view of the mass of literature about roses it would be extremely difficult for any contemporary writer to rebut a charge of plagiarism as defined by the *O.E.D.* Incidentally the dedication of this book is a plagiarism from a famous author, but I much doubt whether it will be traced by readers.

For giving the final touch to the story of Mrs Gore I have to thank Lord Arran and John Gore, CVO.

For my part I acknowledge with humility and thanks all that I have read and absorbed from past writings and on which my own practical experiences have been founded.

I am particularly grateful to two old friends, famous as rose growers and as hybridists: Jack Harkness, whose thoughtful mind brought to the surface the doubts forming in my own about our modern roses, and perhaps more particularly, the question of just how serious is the incidence of the diseases to which they are prone. And Sam McGredy, who, in just over twenty years, has earned the description by Dr D. G. and J. P. Hessayon – 'of having joined the ranks of Europe's great hybridists and whose record no other British breeder can match', for making so freely available to me his views about the present and the future of the rose.

It has given me much pleasure that Anthony Huxley, who, over twelve years ago, in another capacity, edited the first edition of *Roses for Enjoyment,* has with kindness and with wisdom assisted me when doubts and difficulties have arisen in my writing of this present book.

Mr P. F. M. Stageman, the librarian of the Royal Horticultural Society, after a similar interval, has again earned my gratitude – it is most willingly acknowledged, as well as that due to the books in the Lindley Library.

Mr T. D. F. Barnard, Deputy Chief Librarian of the East Sussex County Council, was a most enthusiastic helper in my researches about Mrs Gore and in the provision of unreadily obtainable books. My thanks are offered to him and to the staff concerned. The former provided me with *Larousse – Dictionnaire – Encyclopédique,* for the discovery of which, as a source of biographical information, I am indebted to Elizabeth Willis, to whose husband I owe so much.

There is another library I wish to thank: it is that of St Augustine's College, Westgate, Kent – where I spent a most profitable week.

For helpful information of various kinds I am very grateful to Hilliers of Winchester, Murrells of Shrewsbury, Mattocks of Oxford. And to Elizabeth Churchill, Julia Clements and Violet Stevenson in the 'field' of flower arranging.

For the majority of the illustrations in colour I am indebted to Harry Smith, with whom I had scholastic connections, whose recent death has given great sorrow to me and is a sad blow to all connected with him in the gardening world.

I am also very grateful to Ernest Crowson for rescue operations as regards others. Anthony Tree has provided the pictures taken in my own garden and I am much pleased that one of them has been adopted by the publishers for the dust cover. The line illustrations by Denys Baker delight me.

I again thank my wife for all her help and patience: she will be glad that this is my last book. So will be Leonard Turner, secretary of the Royal National Rose Society, the library of which I have so freely and thankfully used as well as the extensive information as to the current availability in the United Kingdom of the varieties discussed. Lesley Turner was good enough to celebrate her 'two-one' degree by examining catalogues and checking my arithmetic.

And in the context of the Society, I wish also to thank the, if I may say so, very knowledgeable contributors to the rose annuals, whose names appear in the Bibliography.

Recognition and thanks are much overdue to Mrs Rae Rigg for her typing and, in that particular, for her clever and invariably correct interpretation of the ill-prepared manuscripts of *Roses for Enjoyment* and of this work.

And to Ernest Sayers for his highly skilful and ungrudging work in my garden for long hours each Thursday, but for which these two books could not have been written.

There are two other friends to whom I owe much gratitude. They are Ernest and Joan Kleinwort, whose garden, Heaselands, is famous. Having read the synopsis of this book, even before the publishers, they gave me great encouragement to write it. Whether, in the result, they feel that their characteristically kind action has been justified, one has yet to learn or may never know.

How right was a colleague who just on forty years ago said that when the present author has a problem, the whole world had a problem. Most of the world seems already to have been thanked (here, or in Appendix B), but I now offer gratitude to the remainder.

Hobbits
Cuckfield
Sussex
1975

INTRODUCTION

I do not much like the title of this book, notwithstanding that it is founded on the new classification of roses adopted by the Royal National Rose Society and by other countries, including the United States, which has accepted it in principle. At most one can only claim that *Wild* is more understandable than *Species*, because that in fact is what it stands for and, indeed, describes them exactly. To those familiar with Wilkie Collins's *The Moonstone*, the title *Sergeant Cuff's Roses* might have aroused interest: seemingly the Sergeant was at his prime *c* 1868. Such a title, although it may have titillated the horticultural palates of some gardeners, might be too esoteric for a more general appeal. Moreover, there is no evidence, and this would have appealed to the Sergeant, that while he grew moss roses, he was interested in the wild varieties.

A similar objection imposes itself against what could be a currently attractive title, *Victoriana in the Rose Garden*. This is especially unfortunate for me, because beyond that period I do not, in general, propose to go. It is true that, unknowingly, I enjoyed the first two years of life under that 'Dear and Honoured Lady', but I am unable to recollect, nor does research reveal, that the Victorians in general had any popular interest, garden or otherwise, in the wild roses.

The adopted title, however, does with all its imperfections seek to cover, with all my ignorance, what I think I know. The measure of this ignorance may be that my interest in roses did not begin until the early 1950s, when work and health made daily journeys to London inadvisable, so that I became a strictly week-end gardener and decided that roses were the answer to the problems of a garden. Inevitably I bought hybrid teas and polyanthus (to become floribundas). It is very doubtful whether at that time, apart from knowing that the dogroses in our hedges were wild roses, I had even heard of *species* roses, still less of any other kind of roses except, perhaps, musk and moss and these only from general reading.

I can, however, date with some precision when I began to take an interest in roses as garden shrubs; it was in 1959–60 when I had the good fortune to buy a sufficiency of land on which to build a cottage and to have a 'medium-sized' garden plus a field, the size of which was quite arbitrarily fixed. I had some idea that it ought to have things in it other than its existing trees and wild flowers. I remember with shame my pathetic attempts to put in it a few wild rose shrubs, selected from nurserymen's catalogues.

Meanwhile the site generally and the garden proper had been, as described in *Roses for Enjoyment*, the subject of expert advice and so to the planting of many shrubs, plants, bulbs and some hundreds of roses. So started the beginnings of the problems – and there are problems – which the beautiful, colourful modern roses produce.

My recollection is that, as part of the creation of the garden as expertly advised, the wild roses were planted with more purpose and knowledge. I cannot, however, point to any specific juncture in time or purpose when an interest in the old garden roses began. You are spared such recollections as: 'I well remember the day in the autumn of 1961, when I bought my first gallica rose.' In any case that kind of thing does not matter: least of all to gardeners who are reading this book for its realities rather than its reminiscences. It does, however, matter to me because I think it right that readers should know the limitations of my own knowledge of the subject and of my short experience, which, in effect, does not really extend much beyond the ten years during which I have collected, and so much enjoyed, just on 140 of the varieties mentioned in this book.

I do think it matters that readers should know that it was not until having begun to grow the wild and old garden roses, with increasing interest and delight, I found the explanation of my own unidentified feelings in the writings of other people.

Graham Thomas says, in his *Old Shrub Roses* (1954):

> But they are an acquired taste: at least, I have found this very true in my own approach to them. They have a colouring and form unique in the realm of horticulture and they are easy to grow, but they do not satisfy all the modern pre-conceived ideas, either in colour or in their limited flowering season ...

To this one must add what V. Sackville-West said in her foreword to that book:

> It may be true ... that some of the old roses demand an acquired taste before they are properly esteemed and appreciated. Not everyone likes oysters ... It bears little resemblance to the highly coloured Hybrid Teas and polyanthus and floribundas of the modern garden. It is a far quieter and more subtle thing but oh let me say how rewarding a taste it is when once acquired, and how right is Mr Thomas when he

implies that they have all the attraction that sentiment, history, botany, or association can lend them.

For my part I would say from my own experience that the foregoing extracts are absolutely true and, if I be a fair sample, the interest of people in roses – in effect, most of the people who are ordinary gardeners – extends to the sentiments, history and associations of the roses which have gone before and, perhaps, not to the botany, necessary as that may be. Accordingly this book has little botany.

Here may I record a most apposite coincidence? Just as the last paragraph was completed, *The Countryman* for autumn 1973 arrived, with an editorial on the Roman mosaic Great Pavement under Woodchester (Gloucester) village church-yard. So precious is this relic that it has only been fully exposed seven times since the Romans left it, *c* AD 400. But we can plant and enjoy, as the Romans did *every* year, a rose which they had in their gardens long before their arrival in Britain.

If we are what we are because of the evolution of mankind in general it is equally true that our contemporary roses would not be what they are but for what has gone before, whether evolved by nature or by the intervention of man.

The search for novelty and perfection goes on in the rose world as elsewhere, so it is hardly possible to accept that it has been finally achieved in the kinds of roses now so popular: one day the hybrid teas and the floribundas will be in a minority like the old garden roses are now.

Fortunately, if we so wish, we can put in our gardens – no matter what their size – examples of the past, not as museum pieces, but as living plants in their own right from their flowers, foliage, fragrance, fruit, grace, beauty and their frailties. Moreover, as will be seen later they are, for the most part, much less demanding of cultural care and attention than our modern varieties of roses.

But here I venture to give another reason why I hope this may be a worthwhile book. It is no doubt true that interest in the wild and old garden roses is increasing as shown by the sales of available varieties, but it must be recorded that UK nurserymen in general, as well as those who specialise in roses, are in business to meet demand at prices which their customers will pay. It is, I am told, an economic fact that in the horticultural world generally the producers are reducing the number of varieties of plants which they offer. This is so in regard to con-temporary roses, where there are few nurserymen currently offering over a hundred varieties of hybrid teas and floribundas. Nevertheless, the total number of plants sold increases yearly.

One can be much more specific about the wild and old garden roses: ten years ago in Britain there were some 390 varieties (excluding climbers) available for purchase by us ordinary gardeners: today that figure is 262. And of those, eighty are available from a single nurseryman only, and, as might be expected, it is not the same nursery in every case. For this reason I confine myself in general to those varieties which can be found in more than one catalogue. If, however, a variety is in one catalogue only, but has outstanding quality of bloom or general

B

effectiveness in the garden and so is worth searching for, then it is included. (Members of the Royal National Rose Society will have no difficulty because the society keeps an up-to-date register of 'obtainability', covering all varieties, old and new; and I daresay that despite the modest subscription, an inquiry from a non-member would be answered if a stamped-addressed envelope were enclosed.) So indeed are one or two which ought not to have been allowed to drop out.

Much of what I have said – which is mostly what other and more experienced people have said – sounds rather evangelical: 'I have been saved, now every other gardener has got to be saved too.' Naturally, this is neither my belief nor my intention, but I do really believe that it is a mistake to write off the old roses as old hat; and that if we do not have even one or two in our garden, no matter how small it may be, we are missing an important something in the pleasures available to us through the trees, shrubs, flowers, bushes, bulbs and all the rest, if we omit living examples of the past in the ever – if slowly – changing world of roses.

CHAPTER I

EARLY HISTORY

The rose is the most widely grown of all garden flowers: currently in the British Isles some 35 million hybrid teas, floribundas, climbers and miscellaneous sorts are bought each year. They are what they are in all their beauty and frailties because of the process of evolution which is an inherent feature of life on our planet.

Accepted evidence – fossils found in Europe, Asia and North America – point to the existence of roses some 30 million years ago. Like man, who incidentally is not nearly as old as that, they have been evolving ever since through natural selection, cross hybridisation among themselves, and by throwing 'sports', some of which have perpetuated themselves. Man, however, in comparatively very recent years has been assisting nature by highly selective artificial hybridisation.

There seems to have been a pretty long gap between those fossils and other evidence of the existence of the rose. It is not until the Minoan civilisation, which was centred on the island of Crete, *c* 2800–1900 BC, that the rose is found represented in jewellery and ornaments, while somewhat later, 1600–1500 BC, it appears in paintings and carvings of that island. It is generally accepted that around that period the rose had spread or was spreading in the countries around the Mediterranean.

Certainly there is evidence that it existed in China and adjacent lands, such as India, and some writers suggest that it was there that man first used wild roses in his garden. Our western civilisation in relation to the garden rose has especially in more modern times gained much from the Far East, but the earliest are thought to have stemmed from Persia.

As might be expected, it was the succeeding Grecian civilisation which brought written evidence about the rose.

Here, however, it may be usefully said that we are dealing with wild roses or as the botanists have it, the *species* roses. Normally, they have five petals, like the dogrose in England and the Burnet Rose in Scotland. Their Latinised and always italicised names (and those of their fellows) are *Rosa canina* and *R. spinosissima*. But undoubtedly over the ages there have been 'double' as opposed to 'single' sports, so it is not surprising to find that the first are referred to in Greek literature by Herodotus *c* 470 BC.

The first reference to the rose is claimed for Homer in his *Iliad, c* seventh to eight century BC, but it is the perfume of the oil with which the dead Hector was rubbed. Additionally, there is an adjectival use of 'rosy' in the *Odyssey*.

I am bound to say that it is a little confusing, if no less interesting, to find one authority saying that there was no Greek word for 'rose', and accordingly the anglicised 'Rhodes' (the island) is not connected with the rose, because its Greek equivalent, *Rhoden*, is a rendering of the Armenian *varo*.

Whether or not the Greeks had a word for it there is evidence that by the fifth century BC, they were cultivating roses in their gardens and using them for decorative purposes, personal and otherwise, on festive occasions. They also produced Theophrastus, 370–287 BC, botanist and gardener, who noted:

> Roses differ in number of petals, some have five, some twelve or twenty, some are even hundred petalled. They differ also in beauty of colour, and sweetness of scent, some are not fragrant. Some roses are 'rough' (presumably thorny) and in the large flowered fragrant ones the hip is 'rough' beneath the flower.
>
> quoted in *Old Garden Roses* by Edward A. Bunyard

Do we here get the beginnings of what are now our almost conventional descriptions of rose varieties? Perhaps critics of modern roses may care to note the reference to lack of fragrance. Anyway, Theophrastus did not particularise the varieties by name. But whatever the kinds of roses the Greeks did or did not have they were, it seems, not noted as gardeners. But the virile and more exuberant Roman civilisation which succeeded that of the, perhaps, more contemplative Greek culture certainly produced gardeners of skill and great lovers of roses. We find the encyclopaedist Pliny *c* AD 77 naming (mostly with 'place' names) and giving elementary descriptions of the twelve roses of his time. Pliny also gives evidence of medicinal use of roses by mentioning thirty-two remedies which they supplied.

Bunyard says: 'very much has been written on the identification of Pliny's roses and one might continue for many pages to marshal the evidence on both sides'. I give his own guesses later on in the appropriate chapters. We have, however, evidence that the Romans, copying as they did so much from the Greeks, made 'bigger and better' and more ritualised use of roses. Market gardens were established near the urban areas to meet the demand. The rose decorations in houses and on persons – the garlands worn on the head – have left us with *sub rosa* as the expression of the confidentiality attached to things said 'under the rose'.

In view of the conviviality of Roman feasts it may perhaps be doubted whether this convention was any more efficacious then than it is now. *In vino veritas* is probably the more appropriate tag.

One thing we can be sure of is that the roses of the Romans followed their conquests and colonisations throughout Europe. Thus they introduced roses to a much greater extent than the Greeks could have done in their colonies, which lay in the countries adjacent to the western Mediterranean.

Neither the Greeks nor the Romans, however, had a yellow rose. The arrival of that colour had to wait on the invasion of Europe by the Arabs following the decline of Rome. The Arabian conquest of Persia *c* AD 700 is said to have led to their adoption of and love for roses and included yellow ones. Thereafter the extension of the Islamic empire to India in the East and to Spain in the West resulted in a two-way distribution of rose varieties between Europe and China, with Persia–Syria (that classic home of the rose), in between.

During the centuries of intellectual stagnation which followed, as Bunyard puts it, 'the crumbling into dust of Roman civilisation' the rose, lacking the gardener's hand, fades from history, and we can imagine that only the hardy and self-perpetuating varieties would be found among the survivors. But here the Roman Church provided, as in other aspects of civilisation, a link with the past through its monastic gardens.

The early church with memories of the rose as associated with the conviviality of pre-Christian Rome doubtless disapproved of that flower, but eventually and, no doubt, inevitably accepted it as a Christian emblem mystic and for its medical values, of which fragrance was considered to be one. What the others were may be a matter for speculation, but many people will remember the collection in the British Isles of rose hips during the 1939–45 war because of their outstanding worth as a source of the essential Vitamin C.

In the Middle Ages we have the Crusaders in the Middle East and evidence that they brought roses to Britain and to Europe. And we find Edward I (1272–1307) adopting the rose as his badge and so it has continued in English heraldry, coins, stamps and so on. It even gave the name to the Wars of the Roses.

And so we pass on to the Renaissance – the reawakening, the rebirth, with its culture, art – in the widest sense – and the widespread use of printing. In horti-culture, while grafting of plants was well understood – possibly by the Greeks, certainly by the Romans – the production of new rose varieties by seed did not come essentially until early in the seventeenth century. Thereafter there was, so to speak, no holding them and the writings of the old herbalists begin our sources of information.

Gerard, whose king, William III, shared Mary's genuine taste for gardening, mentions fourteen roses in his *Herbal* (1597). Two hundred years later there were ninety according to *A Collection of Old Roses from Nature* (1799) by Mary Lawrance: numerous herbals and gardening books were produced during that period, but Miss Lawrance's was the first illustrated book devoted solely to roses. By 1820 one Roessig was describing 121 varieties.

Here we overlap with the 'redoubtables': the 172 coloured plates of Redouté in *Les Roses*, fortified by the descriptions of Thory and inspired by the Empress Josephine, were issued in 1817–24. Her collection of roses at Malmaison was formidable and despite the Napoleonic Wars was gathered by Dupont (see page 74), director of the Luxembourg Gardens in Paris and by Kennedy, an English nurseryman, who despite hostilities could come and go between the two countries with his rose plants and his skills.

The Empress had a rival collector in the Countess of Bougainville (see also under bougainvillea – a deciduous climber of the Mediterranean coasts). With this additional spur it is not surprising that the Malmaison collection included over 250 varieties.

One reads that thereafter roses were very much in the hands of the nurserymen, some of whom produced erudite and comprehensive catalogues, while the number of varieties offered went on increasing. We find that the index of varieties by my fellow plagiarist Mrs Gore (1838), who wrote about French roses, contains some 1,500 entries, but these I imagine include alternative names, as the *Catalogue descriptif ... du Genre Rosier* of Prévost (c 1830) notches only 880. In fact these are only a small sample of the evidence that seed propagation of new varieties was now on a grand scale and that the dominance of French roses throughout the nineteenth century had begun.

However, Mrs Gore wrote:

> Although the present work pretends to treat only of rose culture as practised by the French, it would be unjust to pass over wholly without notice the remarkable varieties obtained in our own country. A list of the finest roses, of unquestionable English origin, is therefore subjoined; which the lapse of a few years will probably enable us to double in extent.

The subjoined list totals seventy-one.
I am unable to forbear from adding what follows the list:

> The most esteemed kinds of old roses are usually sold by nurserymen at fifty shillings a hundred: the finest French, and other new varieties, seldom exceed half a guinea a-piece. The average price of roses is pretty nearly the same in France; but from the more abundant creation of varieties, new roses pass more expeditiously to the price of old.

To this I add that the sixpence and half-guinea of 1838 in contemporary values would be twenty and over 400 pence.

Mrs Gore's list contains quite a number of varieties prefixed by 'Rivers'. Thomas Rivers's *Rose Amateur's Guide* (1837 to the tenth edition in 1877) is typical of the erudite and comprehensive catalogues referred to above. True it contained only, on my calculations, something over 150 varieties, but it is equally true that the nursery firm which a Thomas Rivers founded in 1725 at Sawbridgeworth in Hertfordshire is still in business and still selling roses. William Paul's *The Rose Garden* (1842–72) is another classical example of nurserymen's writings, in which he deals with, *inter alia*, well over 700 of the then commonly recognised varieties.

This is as far as I think it is necessary to go in what I admit to be, by scientific and esoteric standards, a jejune description of the historical background to the wild and old garden roses, which are commercially available to us today. It will have been noticed, perhaps critically, that in these introductory pages I have not, apart from an illustrative example (page 20), mentioned the name of any variety even among those in the historical past. The reasons are complex: I do not wish to confuse readers by naming undescribed varieties; on the other hand I want if possible to approach what is, as I see it, a highly complex subject, in an interesting and logical way. A course I highly commend to those who, if they reach the end of this book, find that they would like to go further into the historical background and also into the botany, is to read the books mentioned in the Acknowledgements. A practical point: there are the libraries of the Royal Horticultural Society, the Royal National Rose Society and the public (local and county) libraries.

Yes: I realise that I am becoming more and more evangelistic, but there is, I feel, so much pleasure available if one has the will to go on and read on.

CHAPTER 2

WILD ROSES AND THEIR CLOSE RELATIVES

Under this heading are included what the botanists classify as *species*, that is, a group containing individuals agreeing in some common attributes but differing only in minor details, eg *R. spinosissima*. And also their sports and their immediate hybrids, whether created by natural crossings between one another or created by man, including those he has produced by marrying wild with other kinds of roses such as the hybrid teas, floribundas and old garden roses.

Compared with the many thousands of rose varieties produced over the years, the number of wild species are very few indeed: most authorities seem to put the number at about 150. Of these, relatively few – mostly for technical reasons – have been used by man in his hybridisation of new varieties. Perhaps of greater interest is the fact that no native wild roses are found south of the Equator. I do not recollect that I have come across any ecological, scientific or botanical explanation of this fact.

The descriptions of the varieties which follow are grouped for garden convenience, under their main flowering period. They are spring; 'midsummer' (actually about six weeks from mid-June); July and August; and those which give their blooms recurrently. The hybrids and their like follow under the heading of their wild forebear: some wild roses are climbers and they are therefore dealt with in Chapter 10.

The great majority of wild roses carry single flowers: for many people this is one of their attractions because they like to see the stamens. Another very attractive feature is the heps which many provide as compensation for giving flowers during one period only, but heps are by no means confined to the singles. Rose heps vary in size, shape and colour almost as much as the flowers do and to most people they have a beauty all their own in later summer and in autumn. Foliage is an essential feature of a rose bush as it is for any other plant, and we shall see that many of the wild roses have leaves of shape, colour, daintiness and grace never seen in our sophisticated modern roses.

Here, I think, it is appropriate to say a word about those which flower once and are eschewed on that account, especially as this so-called blemish is also urged against the old garden roses too. We gardeners are a little inconsistent. We happily accept other shrubs which flower only once, to name a few – azalea, rhododendron, mahonia japonica, senecio, viburnum tomentosum, lilac and philadelphus – why do we single out this feature as a special blemish of certain kinds of roses? Perhaps, since the arrival of the China rose early in the nineteenth century, we have been spoilt?

But do we tend to concentrate on the flowers and fail to take account of the other features of beauty which the once-flowering roses may also offer? In short the rose bush is in essence a shrub and is entitled to be looked at as a whole like any other shrub.

Certainly, a statement that the wild roses fit well into the contemporary wild garden is quite true; so is one that they can fit happily in a general shrubbery. What is less true is the somewhat general belief that they are too large for the average garden, let alone a small one. The particulars given about height and width – the latter in my view being the more important – will show that while there are those reaching 10ft × 10ft and more, there are many more of average size around 5ft × 5–6ft; indeed there are quite a few which do not exceed 3–4ft in height and they all can be limited to almost any desired width.

After the foregoing massive 'starter' we can now get down to the meat, which also shows, where known, the roses' age, as well as other particulars. I shall simply add that throughout this book, when 'parentage' of any variety is given, the name of the seed parent is given first.

SPRING FLOWERING

R. ecae is a small dainty shrub 5ft × 4ft giving, in late May, brilliant but small buttercup-yellow flowers, oddly scented, all along its slender, arching brown branches. The heps are small, red and globular, but some authorities say they do not come as freely as the flowers. It is suggested that it requires very good drainage: given that, and the shelter of a south wall, it can attain 8ft. It comes from Afghanistan and was brought to the UK in 1880 by Dr J. E. T. Aitchison who served as an army surgeon in the Afghan war of that time. He named it after his wife's initials E.C.A., and has made rose writers mad ever since by not revealing what the 'E.C.' stands for. Until 1940 it was sold in America as *R. primula*. Personally, I think its interest lies from **Golden Chersonese**, first available in 1970 and produced by E. F. Allen – an outstanding scientific expert on, and an amateur grower of, roses – in conjunction with Canary Bird. As the illustration on page 104 shows, it is smothered with deep buttercup-yellow blooms. They come with a sweet fragrance in late May and early June and are supported by plentiful small matt foliage on, as might be expected, reddish arching branches. It arrived in my garden in 1973 and flowered (two blooms) in that year.

Canary Bird referred to above is, I fear, typical of the difficulties which can beset the experts and indeed writers about roses. It is generally accepted that it is a hybrid. But what of? Here are a few extracts:

> Probably *R. hugonis* × *R. xanthina*.
> A hybrid, perhaps *R. hugonis* × *xanthina* or *spinosissima*.
> The parents of this hybrid are almost certainly *R. hugonis* × *R. xanthina*.
> ... probably derived from *R. xanthina spontanea*.
> Both this and the double form *R. slingeri* (*R. xanthina*) ...
> *R. xanthina spontanea* ... sometimes known as 'Canary Bird Rose'.
> *xanthina* ... Unlike 'Canary Bird' which is sometimes called *R. xanthina spontanea*.
> *xanthina spontanea* ... having been overshadowed by 'Canary Bird'.

Having got ourselves down from this wall it seems best to get on with what matters: the rose itself. Without doubt it is one of the most popular wild shrub roses – it is stocked by well over twenty nurserymen – and comes from northern China and Korea. In size 6ft × 6ft, it gives largish flowers of its name colour on and along rich brown stems, which also carry bright green leaves, small and fern-like. It is said to be subject to 'die back', which I have not experienced, and to do better on well-drained soils. When it produces heps (I had one in 1973), they are blackish. I have had flowers as early as 24 April, but the first week in May is when it is usually at its best.

R. hugonis was found by a French missionary, Father Hugh (or Hugo) Rose (or Scallan) and brought to Europe *c* 1900. It grows to about 7ft × 6ft and is another very popular early buttercup-yellow one, with fern-like leaves. It carries a mass of flowers and normally they are well in evidence by mid May. Some people find that it dies back (perhaps through lack of resistance to frost or because it is said not to thrive in soils of high fertility or poor drainage). I had one and I have not renewed it. Others say that when it is good, it is very good, and I am prepared to believe it. But far superior in my garden and in many others is its cross with *R. sericea* which gave:

R. cantabrigiensis to Dr C. C. Hurst in the Cambridge Botanic Garden in 1931 during his work on the genetics of the rose. It has a much stronger constitution than *R. hugonis* and can match it in wealth of flowers (they are somewhat paler) and foliage. But it is superior in the shapeliness of the blooms and, particularly, in growth, the average of which is said to be 'medium-sized' or 7ft × 7ft. My own, after ten deliberately unattended years, measures 17ft × 17ft and has not an inch of dead wood, while it sends up a new shoot almost yearly. As to this, one can only refer to what is said on page 56. With me it is usually out by 21 May. Orange heps follow in late summer.

Headleyensis is another hybrid from R. *hugonis* and was obtained *c* 1920 by the distinguished botanist Sir Oscar Warburg, in his garden at Headley, near Epsom, by a crossing thought to be with R. *spinosissima altaica*. It is included because Graham Thomas says:

> This vigorous and healthy plant has the general ferny appearance of the parents, as one would expect, with particularly handsome creamy yellow single flowers. Very fragrant. I consider this is the most ornamental of all the hybrids of R. *hugonis* ... its wide flowers, graceful growth, and clear soft colouring make it an important garden plant, and it is amazing that it has remained so long in obscurity.

This commendation is echoed in the catalogues of two rose growers whose opinion I value.

Its growth is put at 9ft × 12ft and it is abundantly flowered by early summer.

R. primula, the so-called 'Tien Shan Rose' in the USA and the 'Incense Rose' in Britain, comes from Turkestan and northern China. From 1891 to 1936 it was, according to Shepherd, confused with R. *ecae*. It was introduced into Europe in 1910 where it was also known as the 'Incense Rose' because of the rich aroma from the young reddish-brown foliage which is particularly noticeable on damp days (and when crushed). The leaves may have as many as fifteen leaflets and the flowers, opening usually in mid May, are very much like those of the primrose but fade to white as they grow older. Small reddish heps follow: they are not very conspicuous.

After this rather solid mass of spring yellows, beautiful as they are, it is pleasant to be able to change the colour and, indeed, the continent too.

R. woodsii fendleri is, as the writers and catalogues say, 'the most beautiful and most important form of this species [R. *woodsii*] and a truly first-class garden shrub'. It comes from North America where it grows from British Columbia to Mexico, taking in Alberta, Texas and Iowa to Oregon. A most pleasing graceful variety, with greyish leaves and clear, soft, lilac-pink flowers with cream stamens, which come very early in the spring and are followed by bright sealing-wax red heps, the size of marbles, persisting long into the winter – birds permitting.

R. californica plena. The wild form is a native of North America, growing down the west-coast areas from British Columbia to lower California; its semi-double blooms, 2–3in, are a rich pink, but fade to purple. Reaching 6ft × 6ft, the foliage is fern-like, arching and very graceful. Normally flowering in late spring, it can go on into July. A good garden shrub.

And now, at last but not least, we come to the *bonne bouche* of the spring flowers, the 'Scotch Rose'; whoever heard of Scotland being either last or least? So here follows that 'Scotch Rose' or 'Burnet Rose' and those available of her numerous progeny:

R. spinosissima. That dark thread of confusion which seems to run so perniciously and ubiquitously through the world of roses is here too. *R. pimpinellifolia* has been used as an alternative for what those who use it, or the two together, have thought to be very good reasons. *Spinosissimus* is the Latin for 'closely beset with thorns'. *Pimpinellifolius* means 'with leaves like *pimpinella*'. The latter, anglicised to pimpernel, is a small annual found in cornfields and waste ground with scarlet (also blue or white) flowers, 'closing in cloudy or rainy weather'. So now you at least know, and to little purpose, why the combination is sometimes used and why for us ordinary gardeners a bit of plain Scottish or English is best. However, I have used *R. spinosissima*, which I can neither pronounce nor spell unaided, as being the better known of the two.

The wild rose itself is by no means confined to Scotland, any more than the 'English' dogrose is found in England only, and has perhaps the widest distribution and therefore, correspondingly, the widest variations, especially in height. In UK gardens this is put at 3ft, but in a habitat of sand dunes, 9in is rarely exceeded. In other countries, which range from Iceland to Siberia and to the Caucasus and Armenia, they are said to attain heights of up to 6ft. The flowers, in May and June, are white or pale pink, small, but with 'an exhilarating fresh scent – like lily of the valley in its revivifying purity', and are produced in very great profusion. They give round, brilliant maroon-black heps, whose autumn display adds to that of the foliage, which takes on colours such as grey-brown, plum, dark red, yellow and orange. No dimensions are given for width of growth as it and its progeny produce, most vigorously, so many suckers that they call for checking in the average garden.

Although it is the 'average' garden for which I am writing, I record on my own experience, with regret, the severe diminution in the number of available variations and progeny. In the mid nineteenth century, Scottish nurserymen listed 200 plus; in England, William Paul offered seventy-six. Come about the middle of the twentieth century (1964) Graham Thomas could describe only twenty-six and now on applying my test of availability (see page 17), I can include only eight. Here they are:

R. altaica also known as *R. grandiflora, R. sibirica, R. spinosissima baltica*. Taking its name from where it was found – the Altai Mountains, Siberia – and introduced into the British Isles in 1820, it is, taken as a whole, a larger and better garden edition of the Burnet Rose. The height is 5–6ft; the flowers, creamy white with maroon-black heps. The prickles are larger, but fewer. The suckering and upright habit should make a fine hedge: it does. The heps are black.

— lutea maxima 'one of the best single yellow roses' has vivid canary-yellow flowers which go very well with the bright and rich green foliage. Height about 5ft. Experts say it could be a hybrid with *R. foetida*. A very fitting companion to *R. altaica*.

— Double White which might have been known as 'William IV' or 'Duchess of Montrose' grows to 4–6ft. The double flowers, with longer petals than customary in the group and not opening so much, can be goblet-shaped; in particular they have the wonderful fragrance of the Burnet Rose itself.

THE HYBRIDS OF THE BURNET ROSES

Williams' Double Yellow sometimes called 'Double Yellow' or *R. spinosissima lutea plena* or 'Old Double Yellow Scots Rose' or (in the Western Highlands) 'Prince Charlie's Rose'. Raised, it is said, in 1828 by John Williams of Pitmaston, near Worcester (who also raised pears), apparently from a cross with *R. foetida*, whose fragrance it reproduces in its 'loosely double, bright yellow flowers', which 'have a bunch of green carpels in the centre'. A blemish is that the blooms die badly, in that the petals stay on the plant for too long after the flower is dead. It has the other characteristics of the Burnet, but grows to about 4ft.

— harisonii: *R. foetida harisonii*, 'Harison's Yellow'; *R. lutea hoggii*, 'Hogg's Double Yellow Briar'. These 'other names' show the confusion which exists as to who raised the rose in New York and whether in 1830 or 1838, but they conceal the confusion as to whether or not this rose is the same as 'Williams' Double Yellow' and about which Shepherd's *History of the Rose* devotes some 1,200 words. Bunyard says that 'Harrisonii' [*sic*] is sometimes confused with the 'Persian Yellow' (*R. foetida persiana*). O that dark thread, but it is all good clean fun.

I follow Graham Thomas, who regards those green carpels of 'Williams' Double Yellow' as conclusive against the yellow stamens of *R. harisonii* and accordingly accepts the latter as a different variety. Therefore it was raised or it originated in the garden of George F. Harison, an attorney of New York City *c* 1830, and probably it was another seedling from *R. spinosissima* × *R. foetida*. It certainly has the fragrance of the latter as well as the rich green foliage and brilliant, sulphury-yellow semi-double flowers. Its upright rather sparse growth reaches 6ft and the flowers are well spaced along it. Graham Thomas says they 'make a very gay sight'.

— Stanwell Perpetual is a *R. spinosissima* cross with *R. damascena semperflorens* (the Autumn Damask, qv). It has foliage – small greyish leaves – like that of the Burnet Rose. The flowers are blush-pink which in heat pale to near white. They are at their best in midsummer but begin in the spring with quilled and quartered petals, come recurrently, with the best display in midsummer.

Raised at Stanwell in Essex and put out by a nurseryman named Lee of Hammersmith in 1838, it fully justifies Graham Thomas's 'most treasured possession, and is likely to remain in cultivation as long as roses are grown'. They are rightly widely available.

To those who find themselves much interested in the spring-blooming Burnet Roses, I would commend from my own experience **Falkland**, a pink with heps, 4ft; **Hispida**, with large white flowers rising to 6ft; **Ormiston Roy**, which grows to 4ft and carries yellow blooms; and **William III**, a crimson-purple with heps, at only 2ft. They are all obtainable from one nurseryman only.

We end 'the flowers that bloom in the spring' on, for reasons discussed in Chapter 13, what I regard as an important and hopeful note.

Between 1937 and 1954 Wilhelm Kordes, the German hybridiser, produced from crosses between some of the R. *spinosissima* variants and some modern roses, chiefly the HT Joanna Hill. Seven in all, their names all begin with *Frühling* (spring). Two of them are quite outstanding, both in general effect and in the quality of their blooms: they are readily obtainable and although one of them usually flowers recurrently I include it here for convenience:

— **Frühlingsgold** (1937) from Joanna Hill (HT) × R. *spinosissima hispida* is, in my opinion and that of Graham Thomas, a superlative plant which can hold its own in charm, fragrance, freedom of flowering, and growth with any flowering shrub. 'At the peak of its flowering period there is nothing more lovely in the garden.' This is praise indeed. The near-single flowers of butter-yellow (see page 31) have an ubiquitous fragrance and show beautiful stamens. They are carried along large, arching, well-leafed branches. Sometimes, but not usually, it can produce, as in 1973, a small September crop of flowers. Rightly, readily obtainable. Its normal dimensions are 7ft × 7ft.

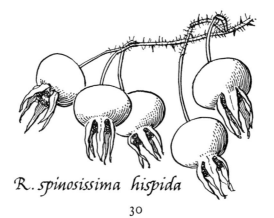

R. spinosissima hispida

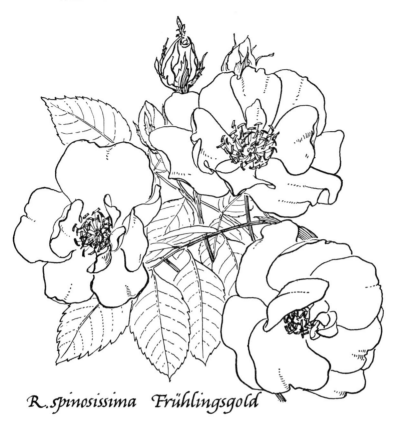

R. spinosissima Frühlingsgold

— **Frühlingsmorgen** (1941) was obtained from E. G. Hill (HT) × Cathrine Kordes (HT) crossed with *R. spinosissima altaica*. The flowers, at every age very beautiful, are a clear rose-pink with a pale yellow centre, and have an outstanding attraction (as page 33 shows) of maroon stamens. This colour is reproduced in the large heps which follow on. Although the leaden green foliage is, perhaps, on the sparse side – 6ft × 5ft – this variety too has a strong claim to be considered among the most beautiful of single roses. The early autumn crop is very welcome.

The other five 'Frühlings' seem to be less popular and are not readily obtainable. They are: **Frühlingsanfang**, ivory 6ft × 6ft; **Frühlingsduft**, cream-apricot 6ft × 6ft; **Frühlingsschnee**, white 4ft × 5ft; **Frühlingstag**, orange-red 4ft × 3ft; **Frühlingszauber**, pink 5ft × 3ft.

I have to my joy and complete satisfaction the two outstanding varieties out in mid May, but I have in mind to complete the collection by buying the other five.

THE MIDSUMMER FLOWERING

The wild roses which flower between mid June and the end of July are the largest group available to us. They tend in some varieties to overlap with the first blooms of the modern roses, but they follow on the spring flowers very comfortably.

Anyway, one does not plant them with the moderns. I think the best order to deal with them here is: those native to the British Isles, Europe, North America, Asia, China and Korea and Japan.

R. canina has already been mentioned. In England it is usually known as our native wild dogrose but, in truth, it extends all over Europe and was one of Pliny's twelve roses which the Romans knew. It is so widely distributed, and so able to survive in such varying conditions of climate, soil and situation, it is hardly surprising that groups and colonies, indeed individual plants, show wide variations in their characteristics of growth, armature, foliage and depth of colour. In short a godsend to the botanists. Although he did not use that word the Rev Joseph H. Pemberton in his *Roses, their History, Development and Cultivation* (1908) puts it very well:

> No wonder, then, that some botanists, not being at the same time practical rosarians, ever spending their time in searching for or hearing of some new thing, have found or thought to have found, subspecies of *R. canina* too numerous to mention in these pages – no less than twenty-nine being given by one authority!

Apparently the botanists have gone on beavering away during the past sixty-six years as I am told that the total is now sixty. However this may be, *R. canina* is cultivated in millions each year for use as understocks on which to 'bud' the sophisticated modern roses.

I have, however, a garden hybrid well worth growing:

R. canina andersonii a wide, arching, handsome bush 6ft × 8ft like the dogrose, but the leaden green pointed leaves are hairy on the underside and the flowers are larger and of a much richer and deeper pink. The oval red-orange heps are

---

FACING PAGE

(above left) *R. cantabrigiensis*, the best and most reliable of the numerous spring-flowering yellows

(above right) *R. moyesii*, a famous and vigorous wild rose, with flagon-shaped heps (page 45)

(centre left) *R. californica plena*, the semi-double form of the American native wild rose found from Oregon to Lower California

(centre right) *R. webbiana* is from central Asia, with ferny fragrance in its foliage and flagon-shape in its heps

(below left) *R. foetida bicolor*, one of the two wild roses said to have introduced black spot, but to be the ancestor of our modern roses in the colours it shows

(below right) Frühlingsmorgen, a recurrent-flowering immediate hybrid from the Scottish *R. spinosissima*

R. canina Andersonii

similar to those of *R. canina*. Books describe the rich fragrance as that of raspberry drops. That of raspberries I know – they are only 10yd from the **andersonii** – but I am too old to recollect what the drops smell like. Discovered by Hillier and known before 1912.

R. hibernica or Irish Rose. Mrs Gore wrote:

> The environs of Belfast produce an insignificant shrub, known as the *Rosa hibernica*, for the discovery of which Mr Templeton received a premium of fifty guineas from the Botanical Society of Dublin, as being a new indigenous plant; though since discovered to become the *Rosa spinosissima* in poor soils, and the *Rosa canina* in loamy land.

Two hundred and sixty-six pages later she wrote: 'We have already alluded to the supposed discovery of this rose in Ireland by Dr Templeton.'

FACING PAGE

(above left) Stanwell Perpetual is its name and another *R. spinosissima* hybrid
(above right) *R. macrantha* may be a cross between *R. canina* and *R. gallica*: for the author it is an absolute winner
(centre left) Frau Dagmar Hastrup is (left) a typical rugosa in flowers and heps, each of which was a bloom and (centre right) the typical and wonderful autumn colours of the foliage
(below left) Cardinal de Richelieu, a maroon-purple with a lighter centre and a button eye, is a typical gallica
(below right) Belle de Crécy is a lax growing gallica, cerise pink when partially open, which becomes a soft parmaviolet full of fragrance

C

For these efforts the poor lady earned a rocket for her 'absurd remarks'. In 1954, however, Shepherd records:

> Now accepted as a natural cross between *R. canina* and *R. spinosissima* ... apparently greatly influenced by the fertility of the soil in which it grows. On a poor soil, it closely resembles *R. spinosissima* and rarely exceeds 3 feet in height, whereas on a rich soil, its resemblance to *R. canina* is apparent, and it may attain a height of eight feet.

And to pile Ossa on Pelion, we find David McClintock saying, in his *Companion to Flowers* (1966), in relation to John Templeton:

> He described it as a new species in 1802, thereby winning a prize of five guineas, Irish currency – which came to £5. 13s. 9d. (not £50 as stated in 'English Botany') for the discovery of a new Irish plant ...

The first edition of *English Botany, 1790–1814*, was no doubt the source of Mrs Gore's information. All I can do is to plant *R. hibernica* in my garden in her memory. It has been ordered, this year, from the one nurseryman in this country who stocks it, as 'a vigorous, medium-sized shrub producing delightful, clear, bright, shell-pink flowers 5cm across, followed by globose, red fruits – first found near Belfast in 1802'. He could have added 'fragrant'.

As the walrus said, 'the time has come to talk of many things' – about Mrs C. F. Gore. One charge of her being a plagiarist is in somewhat exuberant language. I quote:

> The book reads well ... However, it furnishes one of the most flagrant examples of piracy that I have ever encountered. All authors of rose books borrow from those who have gone before them [too true, we do]; this is natural; but Mrs Gore went far beyond that. She translated, in most cases word for word, Boitard's *Manuel Complet de l'Amateur de Roses*, published in Paris in 1836. This was done without so much as one word of acknowledgement in the preface or text. Mrs Gore does not seem to have been that typical British gentlewoman of whom one reads in so many Victorian novels.

Mrs Catherine (Grace) Francis Gore (1799–1861) was, of course, the novelist and dramatist who enjoyed immense temporary popularity. Called 'The Poetess', so well known was she that Thackeray parodied her work in *Punch*. She married Charles Arthur Gore, a captain in the 1st Life Guards, at St George's, Hanover Square on 15 February 1823. Captain Gore resigned his commission in that year. Nothing further is known about him.

Mrs Gore, however, has an entry in the *Dictionary of National Biography* of three and a half columns in which her seventy works are numerically listed. The first came out in 1824: *The Rose Fancier's Manual* is No 26. There are three plays, one of which won a prize of £500. She died at the age of sixty-one and was survived by only two of her ten children.

Mrs Gore even figured in the very early days of Queen Victoria's reign: Lord David Cecil says in his *Lord M*:

> The Queen was more seriously concerned about her duties as guardian of social morality. Anxiously she asked Melbourne ' ... whether she should allow Mrs Gore, the fashionable novelist, to dedicate a book to her ... ' Melbourne tells her, he would have a look at Mrs Gore's book, for 'Your Majesty is always right to be cautious in such matters'.

In the light of all the foregoing information about Mrs Gore it would, one thinks, be right to infer that at any rate she knew what constituted a 'typical British gentlewoman as portrayed in Victorian novels'. More importantly she herself seems to have supplied an answer to the charge of committing un-acknowledged plagiarism, in her book itself, *The Rose Fancier's Manual* (1838), under 'Bibliography of the Rose' on page 70:

> More recently, a treatise on the monography of the rose has been published in France, in the *Encyclopedia of Arts and Sciences*, by Monsieur Boitard, from which is derived the greater portion of information contained in the present work.

It is true that M. Pierre Boitard's *Manuel Complet de l'Amateur de Roses* (1836) does not make a specific reference to the *Encyclopedia of Arts and Sciences* of Mrs Gore's statement, but having regard to the concatenation of dates, the fact that Boitard's title page includes 'Paris – à la Librairie Encyclopédique de Roret', and that Mrs Gore was a novelist, an independent objective approach would, one feels, judge that she was in fact referring to Boitard's *Manuel* ... I put myself in that category. And I add that if he plagiarised one of his own works he would not be, so far as I am personally concerned, the first author so to do.

Poor Mrs Gore, I am afraid that inevitably you and your face must remain bloody, but your head may indeed be unbowed. The faces of your traducers, however, will be, if not bloody, very red and their heads, one hopes, bowed low. Moreover, they may be thinking of taking to heart what Melbourne said to the Queen.

Perhaps some enterprising publisher may take a hint from part of the entry about Mrs Gore in the *Encyclopedia Britannica* that 'Some novels deserve to be revived: her *Cecil or the Adventures of a Coxcomb*, 1841, having been reprinted with success in 1927.' What a pity that there will be no royalties payable thereon. And that Mrs Gore did not get her dedication.

R. macrantha, 1823 is a quoted date, but its garden origin is uncertain and no one is prepared to commit himself. The best I can offer is a 'cross between *R. canina* and *gallica*; but if that is so our present plant is some generations removed from the original cross'. For me and with me 'our present plant' is an absolute winner. Three of them grow *à volonté* in my garden through a hedge of *cotoneaster franchetii*. A pleasure of gardening life (page 18). A magnificent rose.

Raubritter, 1936, is at the other extreme in that it is a most useful, sprawling ground coverer (as well as a climber) raised from *R. macrantha* – 'Daisy Hill' (not available) × Solarium (a rambler). It is 3ft high and its branches to 7ft plus across carry clusters of ball-like semi-double blooms, clear silvery blush-pink outside and rose-pink inside. The incurved shape reminds one of the Bourbon roses. I find it invites inquiries from visitors to my garden.

R. rubiginosa: Sweet Brier, Eglantine, *R. eglanteria*. Found in Europe generally, it is 'one of the most treasured of English wild plants', despite the not uncustomary differing views of the experts as to its proper name – we have had enough of that dark thread. To continue my quotations:

> One of the most beautiful of all single pink wild roses, beautifully fashioned and deliciously fragrant; a fragrance that has its richer counterpart in the aromatic foliage. It forms an arching shrub 8ft or more high (and wide) ... in autumn the masses of glittering oval red heps transform it into a vivid spectacle.

R. macrantha Raubritter

My own experience makes me concur entirely with all of the foregoing. The leaves release their fragrance most in warm moist winds, and as these invariably come from the south-west, the south and west of the garden are the best planting positions.

Apart from smaller variations such as La Belle Distinguée, rosy red, and Manning's Blush, blush white, not easily obtainable, we have the **Penzance Hybrid Sweet Briers**, raised by the then Lord of that name in the very late nineteenth century from *R. rubiginosa* crosses – all have the fragrant foliage and heps. The most readily available: Amy Robsart, 8ft × 8ft, a semi-double deep mid-pink, followed by scarlet heps; Lady Penzance, crossed with *R. foetida*, 6ft × 6ft, coppery yellow; Lord Penzance, crossed with Harison's Yellow, with single fawn-yellow flowers and growing to a size similar to that of his lady;

R. rubiginosa   Meg Merrilees

Anne of Geierstein, a very vigorous, fragrant, dark crimson single; Meg Merrilees, a single bright crimson at 8ft × 8ft.

All top quality for garden use from their general effect, but in general they may need watching for mildew, Meg and the Lord and Lady can, on occasion, show black spot.

R. nitida is found throughout eastern Canada and the New England states. As a garden flower it grows to 1½–2ft and resembles the Burnet Rose in habit: suckering and thus increasing the area covered by the reddish stems. These have 'prickles and bristles' up to the deep pink flowers, showing their yellow stamens, which in turn produce scarlet heps. Excellent as a carpeting shrub. The leaves are small, bright and glossy: they have outstandingly beautiful autumn tints only surpassed by those of: **R. virginiana** which is not confined to that State but widely distributed in eastern North America, ranging from southern Quebec to Missouri. It was, however, so it is said, the first American rose exported to England and it came from Virginia, but when? If it is the same as the 'Virginian Brier Rose' described by Parkinson in his *Paradisus* (1629) it was here before that year. Shepherd, however, says in his *History of the Rose* (1954): '*R. virginiana* ... is descriptive of the source of the first plants sent to England in 1724. It is probably the first native American species to be cultivated in Europe ... ' Hillier's catalogue plumps for 'introduced before 1807'. Graham Thomas, wisely, if I may say so, gives no date at all. I, having noted that Virginia in 1607 was colonised by a London company and Jamestown founded, plump for Parkinson: so much more romantic.

A nos moutons: the clustered bright, vivid cerise pink flowers come from the end of June to well into August; their pale centres enclose and expose yellow stamens.

They are the culmination of the slender, erect and richly red-tinted suckering stems and finally turn to 'glittering rounded heps, which last long after the leaves have fallen'. But before those leaves have fallen they have turned 'first to purple then to orange-red, crimson and yellow'. On my own experience I too can agree that 'there are few shrubs in any genera which have such manifold attractions, and it therefore must be reckoned with the very best'.

Scheduled to reach 5ft my bush has made 6ft; reprehensively assisted by a bird, the mother has whelped some 'twenty yards away', so we now have five.

R. virginiana alba may be a counterpart of the above as 'a beautiful white-

R. rubrifolia

flowered rose', but it lacks the colours in its autumn foliage as well as in its earlier stages. It is said that it may be a hybrid.

R. virginiana plena, see Rose d'Amour, page 48.

R. rubrifolia, 'having red leaves', the colour of which 'raises it above all other roses'; they are soft grey-green with a distinct mauve-purple sheen. The clear pink flowers, rather like those of R. *canina*, showing as they do their light yellow stamens from a centre area of white and followed by brownish-red heps (see page 40), come in bunches on practically thornless red-brown branches. The red-brown heps are esteemed by the birds: three of my four bushes were sown by them. The plant as a whole needs barbed-wire protection from the flower arrangers. It grows 6ft × 5ft and in my view is worth a place anywhere in any garden. Two of mine make a charming group alongside a tamarisk, with the pseudo Félicité et Perpétue (see page 122) in the background and the yellow floribunda shrub Chinatown, and Raubritter, in front. It is a native of Europe generally.

WESTERN ASIA

R. foetida bicolor, 5ft × 4ft; R. *foetida* itself, also known as R. *lutea* and Austrian Yellow Brier, is not readily come by, but the unique flame and yellow bicolour, R. *lutea punicea* – the Austrian Copper Brier – is less difficult to obtain. A famous rose known prior to 1590, it is said to have come from Asia Minor via Vienna: hence the 'Austrian'. The single flowers are an intense near-sulphur-yellow at the back and a vivid nasturtium-red in front. Unique and the most startling of all the wild roses, it is responsible for the orange and flame-coloured two-toned modern roses and, as can be imagined, it needs careful placing among the more modestly coloured wild roses. I have also read that modern roses of their colours attract black spot: a warning that R. *foetida bicolor* itself needs watching for this disease is not surprising (see Chapter 13).

R. persiana, the 'Persian Yellow', is also similar in all respects to R. *foetida*, but the flowers are fully double. It was brought to the British Isles (and thus to Europe) by Sir Henry Willcock in 1838, the then British Minister in Persia (Iran). Growing to 5ft × 4ft it was made very welcome and much used for hybridising. Something more will be said about it and its rich scent in Chapter 3.

R. hemisphaerica, a smaller 4ft × 4ft yellow variety has been since 1622, through Sir Henry Wotton, the only double yellow rose of any 'size'. The light yellow, fully double flowers have no fragrance, and in the British Isles they do best on a warm wall, but seldom reach perfection. People still buy it. It came directly from Turkey to the United Kingdom in 1686 via Nicholas Lee, a London merchant and then, after failure, through another of that ilk, John de Franque-ville's imports in 1695. I shall write more of it in Chapter 9 where hybrid perpetuals and pernetionas are discussed.

R. pomifera duplex or *R. villosa duplex, R. pomifera,* Wolley-Dod's Rose. 'A semi-double hybrid of the Apple Rose' – *R. villosa.* To quote – 'this most beautiful species makes a large shrub, fairly compact, up to 7ft high and rather wider ... At flowering time it is not eclipsed in beauty by any other species ... the huge heps ... orange-red to rich plum-crimson, densely set with bristly hairs.' *Duplex* is a semi-double hybrid attributed to the Rev Wolley-Dod, having – as regards the parent – come from West Asia to Europe in 1771. Saving his Reverence, another source (1966) says: 'Lt-Col Anthony Hunt Wolley-Dod (1861–1918) Etonian and regular Gunner ... was a specialist in Roses, who published no less than four works on the British ones. *Rosa Duplex* ... is known as Wolley-Dod's Rose.' The foreword on the dedication page of that source says:

> It was customary for Col. Wolley-Dod, when he was writing the Flora of Sussex, to go to the Natural History Museum and take copious notes from the Herbarium and Library. When he arrived home, he would find he could often not read his own notes ... This may explain how some mistakes got into this particular Flora.

The reader, if he buys it, must make his own particular judgement of *Flora: pomifera duplex*: my opinion, perhaps because it is too near a Bramley apple tree, is that it is not all that good.

R. webbiana came from the Himalayas in 1879. It has slender growth up to 6ft × 6ft – I am afraid that in my garden the upward growth tops 8ft – and with me has formed a wonderful base (see page 103) for the exuberant rambler Francis

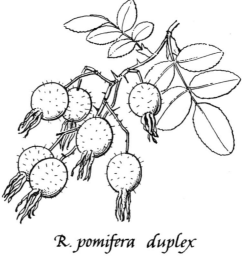

R. pomifera duplex

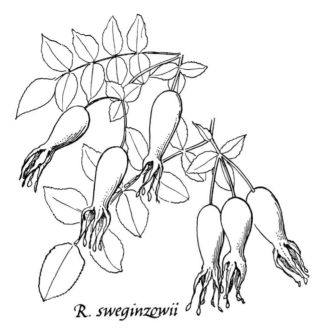

R. sweginzowii

E. Lester (page 117). Its crowds of pale pink single flowers produce flagon-shaped heps of scarlet, which I think has a tinge of orange. The ferny foliage is said to be hard to beat: I think this about the whole plant, and wish that more nurserymen would make it available.

CHINA

What a remarkable wealth of excellent wild roses this ancient civilisation has produced to match its wonderful ceramics, sculpture and culture. They are so many that I am dealing with them in broad geographical order.

NORTH-WESTERN CHINA

R. farreri persetosa, the 'Threepenny Bit Rose', a name which I think accounts for its popularity, despite dimensions of 6ft × up to 10ft. That silver coin is likely to be quite meaningless to people born after 1940, so for their benefit I record that it measured 17mm in diameter and purchased the Mansella cigar which was my pre-1914 boyhood Christmas present to my father. The flowers are of that dimension in a rich pink and are matched by the multitude of miniature leaves, the tiny hairy thorns on the stems and by the very small heps. The now halfpenny rose has fragrance too.

R. sweginzowii has a somewhat difficult name and one that is not identified by the experts. The variety is in the idiom of *R. moyesii,* but it is decidedly, at upwards

43

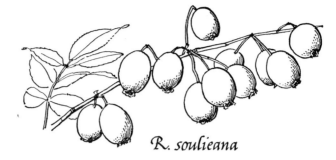

R. soulieana

of 12ft, more vigorous, bushy and worthwhile. The heps are somewhat smaller, yet brighter, and its stalks are much productive of prickles, but it is none the less desirable on that account. It is interesting that Sam McGredy mentions this variety, but not R. *moyesii* (page 140).

WESTERN CHINA

R. forrestiana came from western China as lately as 1922 and is said to be a less hardy relative of the later-blooming R. *multibracteata* (see page 48), The deep carmine flowers are single and scented like those of R. *moyesii*; the heps resemble those of that species and are particularly handsome.

R. soulieana is said to grow 10–12ft × 10ft, and the warning is that it gives its multitude of white flowers on 'a really large bush'. I am ashamed to say that, having just measured mine in a wild garden, it is 20ft × 20ft. But in that location it is worth every bit of that space as the grey-green of the foliage is certainly up to the standard of R. *fedtschenkoana*. My journey of measure was well worth it for a sight of the masses of small round orange heps which go so well with the foliage. It was discovered in 1896 by Father Jean-André Soulié.

R. willmottiae was given its name from that of Ellen Willmott, who wrote the

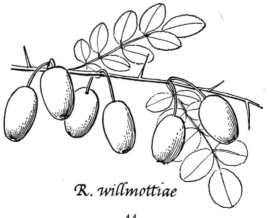

R. willmottiae

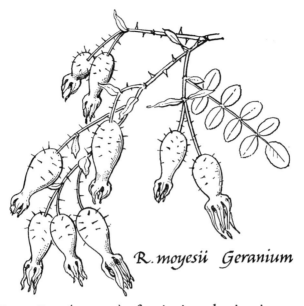

R. moyesii Geranium

well-known *Genus Rosa* (1911–14) after its introduction in 1904. The flowers are lilac-pink with cream stamens and the pear-shaped heps are orange-scarlet. It forms a compact bush 6ft × 9ft and as that 'four-square' doyenne of the Royal National Rose Society, Miss Arabel M. Aldous, has written: 'The even smaller leaflets ... can be used like Maiden-hair fern, but the countless tiny thorns must be rubbed off.'

R. moyesii is, as Graham Thomas has written: 'Perhaps the most famous of wild roses ... which with *R. hugonis* first carried the torch which led to better appreciation of the species roses.' And Shepherd wrote: 'This is undoubtedly one of the most desirable of all rose species in blossom, colour, foliage and fruits.' I agree with both these extracts but would like to include here the *moyesii* hybrids, types and variations.

In *moyesii* itself one has to face up to dimensions nearing 12ft × 10ft, made up of 'elegant lacy foliage' which with the single blooms of 'intense blood-red' plus creamy stamens make 'a high light of the floral year'. It is all that with me, but it is rather awkward in shape and I much prefer **Geranium** of lighter-coloured blooms and which is more suitable for smaller gardens. Raised by the RHS at Wisley, it is more compact in habit, with more foliage of 'fresher green'. Like *moyesii* itself the heps are brilliant, long and flagon-shaped and undoubtedly the most noted feature of the group.

We are told that we owe *R. moyesii* to 'A. E. Pratt and later to E. H. Wilson who brought it into cultivation (1903 or 1908) and named the rose after his missionary friend, V. Moyes'. 'Geranium' did not come until 1938, which year also saw **Sealing Wax** from the same source – a vivid cerise-pink and a form of *R. moyesii rosea* or, if one prefers, *R. holodonta*.

45

R. moyesii fargesii

R. fargesii, like the others above which I have in my garden, is very similar to *moyesii* itself, but it has rose-red flowers and botanically (with which we are not concerned) could be a parent of a very important modern shrub:

Nevada, 1927. Although this is 'recurrent', I am including it here instead of in Chapter 9. As Graham Thomas puts it:

Reputedly 'La Giralda' (HT) × *R. moyesii* it resembles the latter parent in its arching, vigorous growth, 7ft × 8ft ... It is the largest and most dense of the perpetual-flowering shrub roses, well covered with soft green, small leaves, on red-brown branches ... To see an arching branch set thickly with the great, almost single, creamy white blooms, 4 inches across, with yellow stamens, is most satisfying ... The first display is in late May and June; again in August and intermittently onwards.

I echo all that, as I do, perhaps more so, for its sport, **Marguerite Hilling** (1959), a deep flesh-pink with all the characteristics of Nevada.

R. highdownensis, a magnificent seedling of *R. moyesii* raised in 1928 by Sir Frederick Stern in his chalk garden at Highdown, Goring, Sussex. It grows 10ft (with me more) × 10ft. The cerise-crimson flowers and large flagon-shaped orange-scarlet heps are held by some to be superior to those of *R. moyesii*, as well

46

Nevada

as is the more bushy foliage. It is certainly very well worth growing if one has the room, which fortunately I have.

Moving to the Himalayas but still in touch with R. *moyesii*, we have:

R. marcophylla which is described as being of that 'persuasion, but is more graceful'. Grows to 15ft × 15ft plus, but one in the Cambridge Botanic Garden is said to have achieved 18ft × 25ft (see also under R. *soulieana*, page 44). The flowers of warm clear pink 'when seen above the ferny shade of the foliage, are not likely to be forgotten', and are followed by, as one might expect, bottle-shaped heps. I cannot restrain myself from a final quotation from Graham Thomas:

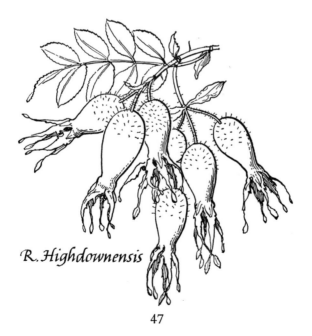

R. Highdownensis

'Few roses have such an elegant poise of bloom.' Obviously, it needs a largish shrubbery or garden, which perhaps explains why only two nurserymen make it available. It is on my list of 1974 acquisitions.

At last leaving *R. moyesii* and all its works, but staying with China, we are offered:

R. sericea (or *omeiensis*) **pteracantha,** is an odd lot and is I believe bought, by people like myself, as much for that as for its garden value. The white flowers are unique in having only four petals instead of the customary five, but much more noticeable, especially against the sun, are the large, flattened, reddish prickles on the stiff straight stems. They can be so very numerous and close that one can see vertical lines of red among the ferny foliage, which finally carries orange-red heps.

R. setipoda. The experts do not seem to have made up their minds as to whether this outstanding rose comes from central or western China. It is, however, in the same family as *R. moyesii* with particularly large flagon-shaped heps, orange-red, which follow on decorative blooms with deeply notched petals of a pale purplish pink, fading to white when they reach the stamens of creamy yellow. They are carried on bristly purple stalks and so are the long calyces; they are said to give a fragrance of pine in contrast to the flowers which offer that of green apples, while the leaves come up with a light scent of sweet brier. Growth is vigorous, up to 9 or 10ft and as wide, the arching stems, carrying large thorns and large distinguished foliage to give a fine bushy shrub rose. It is a pity that more people do not recognise its worth.

THE LATER FLOWERERS

Very few, I fear: very useful as they do march with some of the climbers, but make us wait until July to August/September. Those available are:

Rose d'Amour, which seems to have been mixed up with *R. virginiana*, called *V. plena*, or 'St Mark's Rose', because it was supposed to flower in Venice on 25 April, which is doubted. Also called the D'Orsay Rose because it was used as a buttonhole by the Chevalier of that name: no doubt because the pink flowers have 'exquisitely-scrolled buds unequalled by any for the perfection of their shape'. I have three bushes of Rose d'Amour, perhaps because of its convenient size, which is 4ft × 6ft.

R. multibracteata is another fine garden rose from western China, with a fragrance like that of *R. foetida*. It has numerous lilac-pink flowers, with cream stamens, which produce small red rounded heps. The foliage, on complex twigs, is a multitude of grey-green bracts equalling in size the tiny rounded leaves. The whole is said to add up to 6ft × 8ft, but *pace* the books and with a plea for pardon, mine is 18ft × 18ft.

— **Cerise Bouquet** is the hybrid raised by Tantau in 1958 from a cross with Crimson Glory, giving brilliant cerise-crimson flowers after intense crimson tightly scrolled buds. The fragrance is that of raspberries. A splendid and interesting addition to summer-flowering shrub roses, 6ft × 6ft, which I have yet to grow.

Here I think it would be a good idea to deal with R. *fedtschenkoana* in advance of a necessary separate chapter on the recurrent and so important rugosas with a recurrent variety in the general run of wild roses.

R. fedtschenkoana takes its name from its discovery in 1875 by Olga Fedtschenkenko in Turkestan. It was taken to the Botanical Gardens in St Petersburg (now Leningrad). Has perhaps the palest of grey-green foliage, which grows erectly to 8ft × 6ft. The single 1½in white flowers, showing their yellow stamens and having a similar fragrance to those of R. *foetida*, come continuously during the summer and finish as bristly, orange-red, pear-shaped heps. 'Altogether an interesting and ornamental species' whose beauty goes well 'in contrast with any shrub', especially with R. *rubrifolia*.

CHAPTER 3

RUGOSAS – THE ROSES OF JAPAN

The wild rose of Japan, *R. rugosa rugosa* or the Ramanas Rose in its various forms – sports, natural cross hybridisations, and those man has made as a result of the facility with which it hybridises with other roses – make such a large and important group as to justify a separate chapter. The more so as all those available are, with one exception, recurrent flowerers. And even that exception more than justifies itself by its long flowering period and garden value. The reader may think that I exaggerate the importance of *R. rugosa rugosa*, but remember those Japanese motor cars, cycles, TV sets, radios, oil tankers and fans.

As might be inferred from the geographical position of Japan, the rose is also to be found in northern Asia, China and Korea.

R. rugosa takes its name, I infer, from *rugosus* or rugose meaning 'wrinkled, corrugated', which describes the characteristic of the unique foliage, but which I myself would also apply to its attractive flowers and to those of its immediate variants. It did not reach Europe until 1784, when the Hammersmith firm of Lee & Kennedy endeavoured to introduce it. As Graham Thomas goes on to say: 'It was scarcely a type of rose that would have been given an honoured place then for it brought no new colours to roses ... and the blooms were comparatively

FACING PAGE

The alba Céleste with its grey-green foliage and clear soft pink flowers, followed by heps, has rightly survived for nearly 200 years

50

shapeless. Looking at R. *rugosa* today we find a rose with few faults. It is extremely hardy; it is bushy and it thrives on sandy and other soils, but it is not so successful on heavy clay and chalk. It flowers from the end of May onwards into autumn, bears heps and gives autumn colour. It has a variety of colours and an excellent fragrance.' With all the foregoing I, from my own experience, entirely concur. However, and with diffidence, I am less in agreement with the stated disadvantages: 'lack of form in the double varieties ... the short duration of each flower; its suckering proclivities and excessive prickliness'. Growing as it does, 6ft × 6ft, it is a medium-sized shrub.

I would now add a comment of my own.

It may have been inferred from the previous chapter that the wild roses, with some exceptions such as R. *virginiana*, owing to their growth and the gracefulness of their foliage, lack the elements of substance and solidity; indeed the criticism, if it be one, can also be made about our modern roses. No one can make it about R. *rugosa* and its closely related forms, nor, on the whole, about its hybrids from other roses. Now, once again *à nos moutons*. Unless otherwise stated, they are all in my flock:

R. rugosa typica. R. *rugosa rugosa* is apparently generally accepted as the normal species, with its excellent rugose foliage and carmine flowers, which do not apparently go well with the bright tomato-red heps. A feature which does not worry me.

Alba, 6ft × 6ft; white single flowers, blush-pink in the bud, followed by orange-red heps.

Atropurpurea. R. *rugosa rubra* is a very rich, dark wine-crimson flower with creamy stamens. Why it is sold by only one UK nurseryman, I do not know.

FACING PAGE

(above left) Königen von Dänemark has blooms which are shapely, quartered and button-eyed. A worthy alba queen
(above right) Hebe's Lip: one can see it on the edges of the creamy petals. This damask does not linger long, but leaves a souvenir in heps
(centre left) Fantin-Latour is typical of the roses this artist used to paint
(centre right) Henri Martin, a lovely rose. The moss is clearly shown around the buds and stems
(below left) William Lobb may be a rather gaunt moss rose, but what flowers and how well it looks against the yellow background
(below right) Louise Odier is a beautiful bourbon, whose cup-shaped flowers are full of fragrance

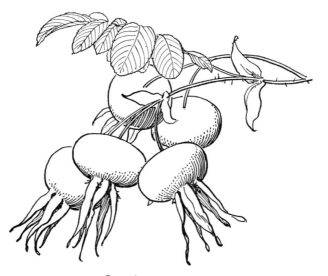

R. atropurpurea

Blanc Double de Coubert is sold by twenty-one nurserymen. There is no accounting for tastes. The pure white flowers, papery in substance, are semi-double and of great beauty, but they produce few heps. It is adjudged of famous outstanding garden beauty (see page 57).

Frau Dagmar Hastrup. To describe this as 'an exquisite single rose, whose clear pale pink is enhanced by creamy stamens and by vivid pointed buds followed with plentiful crimson heps' is to describe a really excellent (5ft × 5ft) plant for every garden. As indeed can be:

Roseraie de l'Haÿ which is hepless, but with double flowers of gorgeous crimson-purple of a rich velvety texture. They look wonderful in my garden (see page 24) with hydrangeas and white old roses. They are fragrant, much more so than **Parfum de l'Haÿ**, which is really not so in spite of its name. The latter is barely obtainable and is prone to disease.

Scabrosa is a variety which the Royal National Rose Society has recognised to the extent of planting it as a frontage hedge at Bone Hill, St Albans. No doubt because of its large and beautiful single, soft rosy-magenta flowers and proportionate heps in great numbers. All are supported by extra good rugose foliage. The whole is of alleged convenient dimensions of 4ft × 5ft; mine, still convenient, is 10ft × 9ft. Due to good Sussex loam or fish manure? (See page 132.)

Belle Poitevine has, with me, semi-double, soft rich mallow-pink flowers on an allegedly 5ft × 5ft bush. Mine, again with humble apologies, is 11ft × 26ft in a right angle. It is not on its own roots, but has extended (to the profit of my friends) through the rooting of its own branches. Said to have few heps, and that is true compared with Scabrosa. I have interrupted this writing to count thirty-nine in 6ft of the 26ft run. What a pity it is that you cannot buy it unless, reading this, a nurseryman may think it worthwhile to stock it: bud-wood from me will be expensive for him.

Now for the second group: the results of crossings of R. *rugosa* with or by other roses.

Agnes, 1922, is the only yellow and, not surprisingly, is raised from × *foetida persiana* (see page 29) through which it gets rich parsley-green foliage. Not growing it, I can only quote dimensions: 6ft × 4ft. The fully double flowers are like some of the old garden roses, 'pompon-like', and their yellow is 'shot with amber and coral'. They have 'an unusual and delicious scent'. It is not so long ago that a friend, wearing it as a buttonhole, defeated me in a challenge to identify it.

Conrad F. Meyer shares a birth year with me, 1899: inauspicious perhaps? Not with me, but certainly so far as my garden is concerned. Growing to 8ft × 4ft, it has fragrant, clear silvery-pink flowers, shaped like those of the hybrid teas and set off by rich green foliage which, however, is decidedly gaunt in general appearance. If it does not appeal to me; it does to other people.

F. J. Grootendorst, 5ft × 5ft, came in 1918 from R. *rugosa rubra* × Mme Norbert Lavaseur. The crimson flowers are like small carnations and come in clusters, but they have no fragrance. I get no kick from it nor from its sport:

Grootendorst Supreme, 1936, of much the same size, but a very dark crimson

Pink Grootendorst

with light red foliage. With another sport I fare much better, as do many other people:

Pink Grootendorst, 1923, whose clear cerise-pink flowers come in bunches and go well with its foliage. No fragrance and not always healthy. But I vote it the best of the three, and so it seems do most other people.

Max Graf, 1919. *R. rugosa* × *wichuraiana* is a prostrate pink, which unsuccessfully I tried to grow in a northern-aspect spinney. Moved to a position in full southerly sun it has gone mad, the creeping roots covering all and more than I want with its fresh green foliage and single pink blooms which come in clusters over a long period but, most exceptionally for this group, in midsummer only. A very good buy.

Lady Curzon, *R. rugosa rubra* × *R. macrantha*. With such parents in 1901, it should be an outstandingly good rose. It is, and upstanding too: 8ft. The single, vivid pink flowers are large, fragrant and of much beauty, enhanced by the cream stamens. They come in great but hepless profusion, and are said to make a most pleasing contrasting effect with the climber **Violette** (see page 119). Altogether it becomes the Marchioness of that 'very superior person, George Nathaniel Curzon' who, in the relevant year, was Viceroy of India.

Mrs Anthony Waterer, 1898, is from Général Jacqueminot (not one of Napoleon's) crossed with a *R. rugosa* hybrid. I have no personal experience with it, but the fragrant, loosely double magenta-crimson flowers come in clusters or singly along arching stems, which also carry dark green foliage and an armature of red thorns. Although ranking as recurrent, its second crop is said not to be a very effective contribution.

R. paulii: *R. rugosa repens alba; R. rugosa* × *R. arvensis.* I have read:

A very low-growing or trailing hybrid ... that bears $2\frac{1}{2}$ inch single white flowers.
A tremendous grower on the flat, it will make a huge bush covered with the large starry white flowers.
A low-growing, mound-forming shrub with extremely thorny, procumbent stems reaching 3 to 4 metres in length.
White, single. Height 3ft. Trailing plant ... with shoots about 12ft long ...
4ft × 15ft.
The shoots grow up to about 12ft long and lie flat on the ground, successive shoots gradually mounding up to 3ft in height.

My shame is that mine shoots up to 18ft and the mounding up to 9ft. 'Please, Sir! it was not me.' My specimen is near the garden shed, which means that when

I am fertilising the roses, it gets a double handful of fish manure (1:1:2) each time I pass it with the full wheelbarrow.

Seriously: it is a first-class ground-covering and garden rose, with a rich clove fragrance and the appearance of a white clematis.

R. paulii rosea is a beautiful pink, but said to be a less exuberant form. Nevertheless, I have not the pluck to buy it. Perhaps it might be wiser to begin with this one:

Sarah van Fleet

Sarah van Fleet. It is something of a relief to turn to this more ladylike shrub, with its generous recurrent production of semi-double, mallow-pink fragrant flowers, supported by *rugosa*-like foliage. My plant is a conformist on height, 8ft, but a decided nonconformist in width, which is 12ft instead of 5ft. In bloom in the first week in May, it has been known to have flowers out in October. No wonder ten nurserymen offer it, but one has given me a warning about mildew: my plant must have heard it, as never a sign do I see.

Schneezwerg. We began the *rugosa* group with a white and so we end it with Snow Dwarf, a *rugosa* cross (?) *R. bracteata*. It came in 1912 after Rugosa alba and Blanc Double de Coubert. Always in flower, with blooms of perfect shape with two rows of petals. Like the Alba, but unlike the Blanc Double, the flowers are followed by orange-red heps which can come at the same time as the later flowers. It is of much the same dimensions as its rivals, 6ft × 5ft, but somehow my two plants do not seem to 'get away' like those of Blanc Double, which on that account and because of its popularity I would put at the top of the three 'whites'.

I hope it will be regarded as fitting that I should here reproduce the end of an article I wrote in a Rose Annual with particular reference to the autumn:

The genus rosa is not noted for the colour of its autumn foliage but there are a few species and varieties which make a decided contribution. At this stage in our walk we see the first specimens of an outstanding class — the Rugosas, which characteristically change their acid-green foliage through bronze to clear yellow. In the case of *R. rugosa* 'Scabrosa', *R. rugosa alba*, *R. rugosa rubra*, 'Belle Poitevine', 'Schneezwerg' and 'Frau Dagmar Hastrup' we add to the collection the most luscious and largest specimens of tomato-like heps. The last-named variety on a bush of 3 feet by 4 feet carried 78 crimson fruits.

In addition to *R. rugosa* 'Scabrosa' and 'Belle Poitevine' this particular shrubbery gives us a wonderful display of heps from a very mixed bag of varieties. *Canina-Andersonii* gives oval fruit in bright orange-red; *R. micrugosa* something quite different in sizeable bristly round fruits. Good too are the orange-red heps of the Bourbon hybrid 'Zigeuner Knabe' and so is the interesting pear shape produced by the variegated blooms of 'Bourbon Queen'.

Then the jungle of the wild garden; one hep from each variety quite fills the pocket, but what variety! First we look at *R. virginiana*: one cannot avoid doing so as its normally light green 'solid' foliage is already the colour of beetroot and is changing to a vivid orange-red, while the short stems are reddish brown and the scarlet heps seem birdproof. One could go on describing the fruits of so many different shapes, sizes and colours — of *RR. multibracteata, pomifera, webbiana, rubiginosa, rubrifolia, spinosissima, soulieana* or, to change the endings, of *cantabrigiensis, highdownensis* and *longicuspis*, or again *RR. willmottiae, moyesii* and such unbotanical names as 'Cupid', a climbing HT and 'Francis E. Lester'. Better still, sit down in the autumn sun and count our store of specimens. Forty-three varieties — all shapes — round, oval, pear, bottle and flask; all sizes from the very small pea of *R. longicuspis* to the tomatoes of the Rugosas and the large pear drop of 'Cupid'; all colours from the black of *R. spinosissima*, the red-brown of *R. rubrifolia*, to the shining scarlet of *R. webbiana* and the orange of so many others.

But this is enough — there is a harmony in autumn and a lustre in its sky.

ENTR'ACTE

We are at an end of the descriptions of the available wild roses and their close relatives. The wide range of their ultimate dimensions has been given and, where appropriate, my own experiences in that particular aspect and, in general, in a garden in the South of England. These include warnings about the tendencies towards the diseases to which roses are prone. It may have been noticed that of the 53 wild species proper in Chapters 2 and 3, only two attract such notice. They are *R. foetida* and *R. foetida bicolor*. Since, rightly or wrongly, it is to these varieties that the incidence of 'black spot' in roses is attributed by some experts, this is not surprising.

Diseases may figure a trifle more prominently in the descriptions of the close relatives of the wild species roses, and of the more distant, old garden roses, so it may help to know that:

Black spot normally does not thrive in built-up or industrial districts; it is in clean-air areas where one has to watch, spray and pray.
Rust can be a killer, but while it may be endemic in some areas (eg, England's West Country has a bad reputation), for the most part spasmodic – I have had it in Sussex only twice in over twenty years.
Mildew is, I am afraid, ubiquitous, unsightly, but far from deadly.

Diseases are dealt with more fully in Chapters 12 and 13.

In the descriptions 'fragrance' has been touched on, even in relation to foliage, for example, *R. rubiginosa*, *R. setipoda* and *R. multibracteata*. Fragrance figures more in relation to the old garden roses, which in general give it very freely. And there are, indeed, wonderful nuances in their descriptions: if these are given, from time to time, somewhat laconically, they are so in no spirit of mockery. I would, however, like to quote from *Roses for Enjoyment*:

> The plain fact is that a sense of smell is a highly personal matter and one indeed which does not necessarily depend on the degree of one's smoking or snuffing, although in general the heavy smoker will not get the same degree of enjoyment from the fragrance of flowers as others do. Moreover, the time of day, humidity of the atmosphere, temperature (whether outdoor or indoors), winds and draughts can all affect the emission of scent from flowers, and the individual's detection and appreciation of it.

I have ventured to add a short glossary of the more esoteric terms used in the descriptions of the varieties covered by this book.

We now move on to the old garden roses – all of which owe their basic origins to the wild roses – and to which a similar method of descriptions has been applied, and in particular refers to my own personal experiences where they differ from those of the experts. In one way or another these garden roses have come from the wild roses and like them, and from them, have their own particular characteristics. These are outlined in each individual group, but in general we can say that they move towards, and indeed arrive at, the characteristics of our modern hybrid tea varieties save, for the most part, in the absence of the spiralled high centres, which are so much admired – or as I and others would have it too much admired.

Wild roses have given their names to some of the groups of old garden roses, the gallicas, albas, damasks, centifolias and Chinas, as well as making their contribution to the bourbons and hybrid perpetuals. Here may I add that these and the rugosas are not watertight compartments: they lead on and intermingle from their predecessors. The general characteristics of the various groups are briefly described in the appropriate chapters.

May I add as a reminder, that for the overwhelming part of us all, we are dealing with a horticultural hobby from which we seek to extract something of the pure joy of life.

GALLICAS

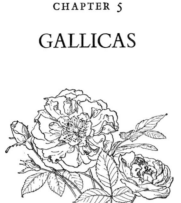

In Pliny's twelve roses of his day (see page 20) are 'Praeneste – Flowers latest of all' and 'Miletus – Late, brilliant red'. Against the first Bunyard puts '? Gallica', and against the second an unequivocal 'gallica'. Had Pliny put pink in front of 'Flowers' there would have been no need for the question mark, as 'Praeneste' could have been *the* Rosa Gallica, which gave the name to what Graham Thomas says ' … are at once the most ancient, the most famous, and the best garden plants among the old roses'. The gallicas have been found wild in France, Spain, Italy, in Central Europe and in the British Isles: in fact where the culture of Rome made itself felt. Why *R. gallica* is so named and has other names – French Rose or Rose of Provins – I leave readers to make their own research among the books named in the Bibliography. But I can at least offer a warning: 'Provins' has the flavour of 'province' which Latinised is 'provincialis', but *rosa provincialis* must not, according to one authority, be confused with the Provence Rose which is *R. centifolia* (see page 77). Another authority says that the name Provence Rose was reserved for the large group of hybrids between it and *R. gallica*. Quite clear? Splendid: you have the advantage of me!

R. gallica grows up to 3ft, but generally of compact growth with double or semi-double blooms. The clear pink flowers come in midsummer. Being wild, they are single, showing the yellow stamens. They are followed by heps containing a rich harvest of highly fertile seeds, which produced in bygone years, as one might expect, various variations and hybrids. This can readily account for the existence of the 'clear pink' and 'brilliant red' forms at the same time as the mauves, purples and maroons produced in the nineteenth century. The stems are

R. gallica versicolor

practically thornless and come very freely from suckers when grown on their own roots.

To continue the above quotation from Graham Thomas: 'They are also the ancestors in part of most other old roses, and their delicious fragrance is carried down through all their descendants.'

We will begin with the older garden forms. The first one, Alain Blanchard, comes aptly to illustrate what is said at the end of Chapter 4, that the various groups mentioned therein have intermingled and interbred.

Alain Blanchard is dated as '1840', '1839' and 'prior to 1825', but it seems to be accepted as a very ancient type from a cross with *R. centifolia*. The flowers are semi-double – nearly single – cupped in shape and showing golden-yellow stamens. Rich crimson to start, but soon changing to maroon shading in a mottled pattern; this in turn changing to purple with a light crimson mottling. The dimensions are 4ft × 3ft; the foliage is interesting and mid green. The stems have centifolia thorns.

R. gallica officinalis 'of practical use to man' which no doubt accounts for one of its other names, Apothecary's Rose, and – stretching it somewhat – to the probability that it was the 'Red Rose of Lancaster'. It is *not* 'the Red Damask'. The light crimson semi-double flowers come rather late in the season and give good heps. Its habit is in general similar to that of *R. gallica* and it adds up to a very good garden rose, 4ft × 4ft. But perhaps its greatest claim to our admiration is its more spectacular sport, the pre-sixteenth-century:

Alain Blanchard

Rosa Mundi or, if one wishes, *R. gallica versicolor*. It is not rating this variety too highly to say that it is 'perhaps the most spectacular of all garden shrubs, when loaded with its gay crimson flowers splashed and striped with blush-white' (see page 62): for the rest it is like its parent, but I cannot resist using it as an illustration of what an odd lot, in a sample of the mass of people interested in roses, we are. In late years the Royal National Rose Society has invited raisers to exhibit at the Summer Show their new, but not at the time commercially available, seedlings

R. gallica officinalis

and the public to vote thereon. In 1972 the most votes were given to a striped sport of the hybrid tea Piccadilly, which was duly 'cover-paged' by a well-known horticultural weekly. Sports do not, as shown in the Glossary, depend in any way whatsoever on the person or firm in whose garden or nursery they occur. Rosa Mundi has existed and given great pleasure to generations of rose lovers over 500 years: compare that with what is said about Piccadilly in Chapter 13.

Tuscany, the 'Old Velvet' rose, is similar in habit to R. *ociffinalis*, and thus goes back to R. *gallica*. The flowers, semi-double, open from dark buds to – what one might expect – velvety maroon, with appropriate yellow stamens.

Tuscany Superb, prior 1848. A dark crimson-purple, growing to 4ft × 2ft compared with Tuscany's 4ft × 3ft, it has larger foliage, larger flowers and more petals, so losing some of the intensity of colour of the stamens of Tuscany, which has to give way to the Superb, and does in fact do so in the popularity stakes.

Conditorum is like R. *officinalis* and Tuscany, but its loose flowers are of rich magenta-crimson with a purple flush, especially in hot weather, and are carried on a slightly smaller plant, 3ft × 4ft.

News, a floribunda 1969 (RNRS Certificate of Merit and 1970 Gold Medal). Lilac Charm × Tuscany Superb. Raised by Le Grice the blooms are beetroot-purple, moderately full (eighteen petals), borne in trusses. Growth: bushy and compact; foliage: medium green matt. Such is the gist of the Gold Medal citation but as to colour I prefer my own description in *Roses for Enjoyment* (1973). 'Described as "beetroot-purple" it is really better than that: I see in it the dark crimson-purple of **Tuscany Superb** and the purplish-crimson of **Roseraie de l'Haÿ** ... Quite a colour break and quite welcome.'

We shall be referring to News in Chapter 13.

We can now move on to the available and more luxuriant varieties. Those outstandingly good, either as garden plants and/or for their excellent blooms are:

Belle de Crécy, *not* 1346, is *une vraie belle*, whose numerous, very fragrant flowers begin with an intense pink freckled with mauve and progress rapidly, especially in hot weather, through violet to lavender grey, sprinkled sparsely with purple and cerise tints. When fully open, the petals are flat or reflexing and reveal a green 'button eye'. The dull leaden green of the foliage makes an excellent foil for the blooms. It would merit the description *une vraie belle parfaite* but for a relatively small blemish, which is that its growth is somewhat lax. However, support from other plants ensures the attainment of its 4ft × 3ft, and it looks at its very best associated with whites such as Boule de Neige (page 93) and Mme Hardy (page 94). Let us follow it with a churchman of equally high quality and of a colour well befitting his cloth.

Cardinal de Richelieu was Minister to Louis XIII for eighteen years and figures prominently in Dumas's *The Three Musketeers*. In the world of roses Richelieu's name was given in 1840 to a gallica hybrid, 5ft × 4ft, with blooms of a sumptuousness unsurpassed in rich velvety purple. Ultimately, the ball-like flowers become a dark purple similar to that of a black grape. It repays the best attention. It also looks extremely well with Céleste (page 69) and Maiden's Blush (page 70). (Historians who are also interested in roses may have noted that Cardinal de Richelieu's successor, the Italian Cardinal Mazarin, has not been accorded the honour of having his name attached to a rose.)

Charles de Mills, also called Bizarre Triomphant, is claimed to be unique, especially in the shape of the flowers which are full-petalled and ball-shaped after appearing to be 'sliced off' in their half-open stage. Its colour ranges from rich, very rich crimson-purple, through maroon and dark lilac to wine shades. Like its class, the growth – 4ft × 4ft – and colours fit well with the strong pink varieties. Of similar dimensions is:

Duc de Guiche, adjudged to be a later variety than those above, but no dates seem to be shown in the books. Shepherd, however, writes: 'Intensive saving of *R. gallica* seeds was begun by the Dutch as early as 1670.' Graham Thomas says: 'This is undoubtedly a more recent variety with a sophistical beauty and perfect petal formation, and comparable with Mme Hardy and Belle de Crécy.' Its colour is crimson-magenta, which becomes veined with purple in hot weather. It has a green eye and may be quartered. The foliage is well up to the standard of the flower.

Francofurtana is the object of somewhat disconcertingly complicated research, but we can record that it takes its place as a very good garden gallica hybrid, 3ft × 3ft, dated 1583 or earlier, with blooms in the superlative class. They are a clear rich pink, which is veined in a deeper shade of that colour – even to purple – appearing in wavy petals which come either in single or double form and finish with heps of turban-like shape. Hence one alternative name *R. turbinata*: others are the Frankfort Rose and, more particularly, Empress Josephine or Souvenir de l'Impératrice Josephine. It is also typical of the confusion which can arise that Shepherd writes: 'The growth of the canes is exceptionally vigorous and to about 8ft', while in the British Isles we think in terms of 3ft × 3ft. The explanation seems to be that Shepherd was writing of Agatha, a variation, known in the US but not available in the UK, and said to be a vigorous grower up to 6ft. Anyway, considering what she did 'rose-wise', Empress Josephine more than deserves a 'souvenir' in our gardens and to be stocked by more rose nurserymen. And that last comment applies also to:

Jenny Duval, about which I also like very much Graham Thomas's comment that the lilac colouring is 'considerably more definite in colour than some of the modern so-called 'blue' roses, when one goes on to say that the fully open blooms give us rich purple, Parma violet, brown and grey in the centre – fading to lilac-white on the edges.' To this one can add that, in hot periods, there are 'quarters' and petals of vivid cerise-magenta. All this is supported by typical gallica foliage and height of growth. Whatever her origin, Jenny has a real claim to have pride of place for the most splendid colouring among the gallicas.

As I have got on to the theme of 'more nurserymen ought to make them available' I will continue with:

Président de Sèze, *c* 1836, which gives us quartered flowers when fully open, rolled petals which show dark magenta-crimson in their centres and lilac-white around the outer edges. A remarkable contrast carried on a broad-foliaged bush, which is extremely suitable for the front of beds because it seldom exceeds 3–4ft.

Surpasse Tout is over-named, but it is a pity that it is to be found at one nursery only, because it is a most worthy crimson-scarlet or, perhaps, rosy-crimson around a button centre, and altogether worth a recommendation for general effect and garden use, as well as having outstandingly good blooms. The latter quality is also to be found in:

Camaieux, 1830. Although healthy, this is not a very strong grower (3ft or thereabout), with arching stems carrying sage-green foliage. Its beauty and therefore its essential attraction comes from the superlative semi-double flower that goes through various stages before reaching its apogee. Beginning with a not very promising bud, the petals move to blush-white heavily splashed and striped with

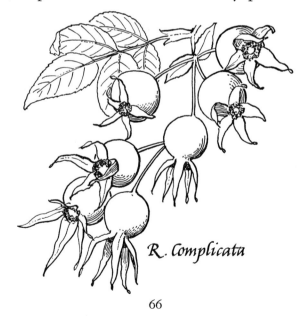

R. Complicata

light crimson; more rapidly, a violet-purple flush takes over. This fades to magenta and then to the pure joy, on the fourth day, of lilac-grey stripes on a white ground, and so ends this strange eventful history ... sans everything, save heps.

Tricolore de Flandre, 1846, follows on Camaieux naturally. Its stripes are somewhat wider and a deeper magenta-purple and the petals are narrower. But it is very much in the same quality class, 3ft × 3ft.

Du Maître d'Ecole, whose flowers are big enough to attract any schoolteacher's attention as they come up to 5in in diameter, so it is not surprising to find the stems of the 3ft × 3ft bush prone to arch, especially as they are aided by large-leafed foliage. The blooms are exquisite, with sweet fragrance and in colour a soft rose touched with lilac which changes to include purple and grey topped off with a shot-silk effect. Add quartering and a button eye to the flatness of the bloom and one has another variety with superlative flowers.

Complicata is a 5ft × 8ft gallica hybrid which is much larger than the general run of the group. It is what I term a scrambler and a clamberer on its performance in my garden, where it gets into large shrubs and over other shrub roses. As far as I am concerned it can do no wrong, because the pink flowers are brilliant in tone, well set off by a white eye which surrounds the yellow stamens *and* they are single. If you have the room, planting it will never be regretted.

The gallicas have yielded in the foregoing a harvest of indisputable and available winners. The following, while being available, are worth consideration as estimable runners-up:

Hippolyte, purple, 5ft × 4ft; **Duchesse de Montebello,** pink, 5ft × 4ft, early flowering and probably incorrectly named (which does not matter); **Perle des Panachées** (Cottage Maid), white with irregular streaks and flakes of crimson, 3ft × 2ft.

I now quote from Shepherd:

Descemet was the first Frenchman to breed roses extensively, and it is said that when the forces opposing Napoleon entered Paris in 1815, Vibert moved some 10,000 Descemet seedlings to his nurseries to prevent their destruction or loss through neglect. The majority were *R. gallica* hybrids.

In 1848 William Paul's catalogue offered 471 varieties. I can produce only 22.

CHAPTER 6

ALBAS

This group, as much as any, goes back very far in the history of the rose and seems to have been one of Pliny's twelve, if one can reconcile: 'Thorn Rose, Petals very numerous, thorny branches of remarkable length' with a potted modern version of the *Alba*, 'Vigorous erect shrubs with a few large prickles ... ' I can.

Perhaps chronologically the albas ought to have come first, especially in view of Bunyard's saying: 'and can be traced through the civilisations of Europe with more certainty than any other cultivated Rose'. But Graham Thomas says: 'the most ancient ... among the old roses', and that is good enough for me. We can accept, too, that it has an affinity with *R. canina* in England and other countries. Moreover, Desportes's catalogue, while showing 1,213 gallicas to my 22, could produce only 112 albas against the 8 which follow here.

Anyway, what there are have hardiness, vigour and happiness under all conditions – whether those be dry, wet, sun or shade – *and* they can hold their own against the roots of other trees. Their foliage has a grapelike bloom and certainly diseases have no terror for them.

As 'availability' is the test for a rose's inclusion in this book, I avoid having to spend any more time trying to trace what the original *R. alba* was like, especially as I have read somewhere that it was a single flower, which it could have been from *R. canina*. But, equally, it could have been a semi-double or even a double (*vide* Pliny's rose) if in fact the original wild alba was, as some authorities say, a natural cross between *R. damascena* and *R. canina*.

For ordinary gardeners like ourselves it really does not matter, but I believe that readers will share my admiration and enjoyment of Bunyard's urbane prose when in the context of *R. alba* he writes:

In attributing the names as below I have referred to the various Botanical and Horticultural works available, and my predecessors will, I am sure, grant me, upon occasion, the historian's privilege of occasional disagreement.

Bunyard then proceeds, as I do, to:

R. alba maxima, the **Great Double White** or **Cheshire** or **Jacobite Rose;** a grand rose of great antiquity. The stems carry a wealth of lead-green leaves in bunches which tend to be mostly at the top, and that can be over 6ft. The blooms are fully double, flat and come abundantly: they have muddled centres, which on opening are creamy-blush, but that changes to a similar tone of white and then to oval heps. The habit of growth mentioned above points to planting at the back of a border.

It is a classical example of the nomenclatural confusion which seems to arise, because not being content with Jacobite and Cheshire it is sometimes claimed as the White Rose of York, the emblem adopted by the Yorkists in the Wars of the Roses. By what seems to me a majority vote, the more probable White Rose was:

R. alba semiplena, but that allocation does not appear to have prevented the horticultural historians from having some lively skirmishes in relation to the probable date when *R. alba* arrived in this country, in view of the known date of that civil war. A war which clearly would never have arisen had the urbanity of a Bunyard been available in 1455.

The essential difference between *maxima* and *semiplena* is that in the latter the flower is nearer to being a single than to a semi-double; either way it has added beauty from the exposure of its golden-yellow stamens against the milk-white of the petals. Has red heps too. This must be supplemented by the probability that it is one of the roses grown at Kazanlik in Bulgaria, for distilling attar of roses.

Céleste takes us from 'ancient' to 'late eighteenth-century'; also known as **Celestial** and an outstandingly good and charming rose in its fresh simplicity. Céleste is perhaps oddly named, beautiful as it is, because it means sky blue, but perhaps this really implies that it is at its best against such a sky. Mine grows between *R. canina andersonii* (page 32) and *R. rugosa* Belle Poitevine (page 54). If she feels out of place, she does not show it. The cool grey-green foliage makes an excellent link and at the same time a wonderful complement to the clear soft pink of the shapely flowers and to the subsequent heps. Flower arrangers would rank it with Fantin-Latour, and I would not dissent from one who said it was 'the most beautiful rose of all'.

Félicité Parmentier, 1836. Few of the albas have more beautiful buds and such exquisite blooms. Grey-green foliage again plays its part in setting off the flowers, which have a full complement of petals. These are arranged in rosettes and have

E   69

graduated from pale yellow buds. The bushy plant 4ft × 3ft is a great help too in the make-up of a first-rate garden rose, which ought to be appreciated as much as:

Königen von Dänemark, 1826, 'Queen of Denmark' to those of us whose German is rather weak, an adjective which cannot be applied to the plant. Without more research than one is prepared to give, I cannot say anything about the Queen of Denmark in 1826. One does recall, however, that in 1863 Queen Elizabeth II's great-grandfather, Edward VII, married Princess Alexandra, the eldest daughter of Christian IX of Denmark. One also does not know whether the particular Queen of Denmark was 'a pearl beyond price', but the rose has been so described because of its extremely well-shaped pink blooms, which just after the bud stage are a unique, intense scarlet-pink, a colour which continues in the centre of the open blooms. These in their turn become a soft uniform pink, when the quartering and button eye are fully apparent. The growth, 5ft × 4ft, is perhaps rather too open and may reflect a hybrid parentage with *R. centifolia* or *R. damascena*.

Mme Legras de St Germain, 1848. I am sorry that this white alba is not more freely available: it is of the same high quality, but not the colour, of Königen von Dänemark and is of somewhat larger growth – 6ft × 6ft. William Paul called it 'a superb White Rose'. The cupped blooms are quite flat and have a regular formation of petals, which are clear ivory-white, but in the centre this is preceded by a flush of canary-yellow. They are carried on thornless arching stems. It is said to be a close relative of another noisette × alba hybrid white:

Mme Plantier, 1835, which is rather better known than its relative, but being outstanding for garden use and general effect, it has somewhat less superlative quality of blooms, although there are more of them. They are pompon in shape, creamy-white in colour and while rated as 5ft × 6ft can, in rich or well-fertilised soils, as mine does, reach into trees and large shrubs, 12ft or more. If one delves among the antecedents of Madame, one will find other contenders with the noisettes – the hybrid Chinas and damasks – as being concerned in the parentage of this very hardy and long-lived rose: one which, were it not completely sterile, might have fathered or mothered some extremely mighty roses.

Maiden's Blush dates from before the fifteenth century. It is very good in its general effect as a garden plant and is popular for the fragrance of the flat muddled arrangement of its blush-pink petals. The blooms are extremely well set off by the grey-green foliage. Called the 'Great', it adds up to 5ft × 4ft. The 'Small' is similar, but less popular, and is shorter by 12in.

CHAPTER 7

DAMASKS AND PORTLANDS

This is another of what I seem to be terming the 'Roman roses'. Pliny had two of his 'twelve' adjudged by Bunyard to be damasks and, more interestingly, he describes one of them: 'Carthage – Flowers in winter'. This I take to be the first reference to a recurrent flowering rose. But from my readings I would say that owing to the different types and nomenclature, the damasks are the most difficult group to describe and, more particularly, owing to the diversity of characteristics, to be assigned their natural parentage. Certainly, they have 'circular' leaves in their mostly lax-growing foliage, which feature can be echoed in the nodding blooms: Celsiana (described later) is, perhaps, a good example of what one may expect – but not always get. Space does not allow me to offer the various suggestions which have been put forward. We must just settle for 'that it goes far back in the history of the rose'. We ought perhaps to remember that in the United Kingdom 'damask' stands also for a colour. The 'wild' *R. damascena* is described by Shepherd as having long, arching, pale green stems, well armatured and carrying small clusters of double blooms varying in colour from deep blush to pale rose, followed by bright red oval heps. Long esteemed for its fragrance, and much grown for making attar of roses, it is available from only one nurseryman in the British Isles. This also applies to the recurrent-flowering:

Quatre Saisons, the Autumn Damask, or *R. damascena bifera*, which produces very fragrant double flowers of poor quality from early summer to early autumn. It qualifies as ancient history – pre-Roman – rather than as garden value, but the following varieties are in better supply:

Blush Damask whose fully double, ball-shaped flowers come in early summer in great profusion on the 6ft × 6ft bush, and its damask-pink is a dark lilac-pink in the early stages. Will grow almost anywhere. As part of the confusion at which I have already hinted, it is sometimes called *R. gallica damascena* or **Blush Gallica**, no doubt because the foliage is of the *gallica* kind. But whatever called, it is a good plant for the shrub border or 'wild garden'.

Celsiana, 1750, is indeed 'one of the very best of the old garden roses', with fragrant flowers and foliage in such happy harmony. Graham Thomas once said: 'I think one can forgive a plant for not doing more during the season if it produces over a hundred blooms in the space of three weeks.' They are all blush-pink after an earlier warm light pink, wide, semi-double with bright yellow stamens. The light greyish-green foliage 5ft × 4ft sets off well the loose folded petals of the flower. It is named after Cels, a French plant breeder who introduced it into France from Holland.

Celsiana

Gloire de Guilan did not come to the UK until 1949 when it was brought from Persia, and where it is another of the attar-making damasks. A clear pink, the flowers open to reveal quartered and folded petals. Again the foliage complements the blooms: it is 4ft × 4ft.

Hebe's Lip grows to 4ft × 3ft and what she lacks in size and in the relative short-ness of her flowering season (what a pity with such a name) she makes up in the number of other names: **Margined Lip, Reine Blanche,** *R. damascena rubro-tincta.* The blooms are nearly single, creamy in colour with crimson around the edges of the petals; they are well set off by the dark foliage and give heps to finish.

Madame Hardy

Ispahan has to be rated highly as a very good garden plant, especially as its flowering period lasts longer than that of any other damask. During this it produces numberless clusters of clear pink, loosely petalled blooms of much fragrance. It has small shiny leaves, with a total growth of 5ft × 4ft. Also, it has **Pompon des Princes** and **Rose d'Ispahan** as additional names and as Ispahan – Rose d'Ispahan – takes its name or names from, now, a province of Persia but formerly the capital of that country.

Kazanlik is mentioned because it appears in four catalogues. Its proper name is *R. damascena frigintipetala* and it is grown in Bulgaria for attar. It has no garden value.

Léda, the Painted Damask, is of most useful size, 3ft × 3ft, and makes a compact plant with really dark green rounded foliage; but it is and should be most esteemed for the beauty of the flowers, which are button-eyed. They begin with red-brown buds, opening to milky white, faintly suffused with blush, while the red tones of the bud change to carmine and remain on the tips of the outer petals: hence, 'painted damask'. Leda is, of course, the lady that laid eggs.

Marie Louise. It is interesting to find that the non rose-growing empress of Napoleon is also remembered in a rose, and a sumptuous one too, raised at Malmaison in 1813, that is, after she had supplanted the Empress Josephine. The

73

flowers are heavy and large, very full-petalled and a uniform mauve-pink with a pronounced button eye; it is not surprising that the stems arch when this feature is added to the abundant foliage, and that the height is only 4ft.

Mme Hardy, 1832. Her husband followed A. Dupont as director of the Luxembourg Gardens (page 22) and he certainly bred a real winner in this white and very fragrant rose, when he crossed *R. damascena* with *R. centifolia*. Personally I would bracket it with Boule de Neige (page 93) as first in the 'any white class'. It certainly has no peer and both varieties are far and away superior to any hybrid tea white. The plant can attain dimensions of 6ft × 5ft. The foliage is dark green. The blooms are of perfect form, with a trace of flesh pink when half open. When fully open, with the outer petals reflexed, they are pure white and of perfect shape (page 73), having a concave centre, but otherwise quite flat. Thomas Rivers said: 'A more magnificent rose does not exist, for its luxuriant habit and large and finely shaped flowers place it quite first among the white roses ... '

Omar Khayyam is 3ft × 2ft with fragrant, flat soft pink flowers of no great size, but which have quartered and folded petals with a button centre. Its real interest is, however, from the name, in that it was propagated from a bush on Edward FitzGerald's grave at Boulge, Suffolk; raised in 1893 from seed which, it is said, came from Omar Khayyam's grave at Nashipur, Persia.

York and Lancaster has other names: *R. damascena versicolor, R. damascena variegata*. I accept from experience that the flowers can be beautiful and think it warrants Bunyard's saying: 'Parkinson's (1629) description of this flower could be shortened, but not bettered. It has

the one half of it sometimes of a pale whitish colour, and the other half of a paler damask colour than the ordinary [damask]; this happeneth so many times and sometimes also the flower has divers stripes and marks on it, as one leafe white or striped with white, the other half blush or striped with blush, sometimes also all striped or spotted over, and at other times no stripes or marks at all as nature listeths to play with varieties in this and other flowers.'

This description should make clear that it is not a splashed and striped rose. But what is not so clear is why it has the name it does. This was apparently given to it, or first recorded, by one Monardes in 1551. Shepherd says:

The history of the York and Lancaster Rose is one of the most controversial of all rose subjects ... Legend has given us many interesting stories concerning this rose, but practically all are traceable to Shakespeare (1564–1616), rather than to a recognised botanist or herbalist and one of little historical value.

My own elementary research among the books listed in the modest Bibliography leaves me thinking that my mentor, Graham Thomas, is getting somewhat nearer than most writers with his:

> No doubt this is the rose which played prominently in the 'brawl in the Temple Garden' between Yorkists and Lancastrians, which factions apparently later adopted *Rosa alba maxima* and *Rosa gallica officinalis* as their emblems.

But I do question the 'no doubt' and the 'later' because I see no reason why the two last named ancient roses should not have been in the Temple Garden (*c* 1455) at the same time as *R. damascena versicolor*. They are in my garden as they are in those of other people, but the last named does need good rich soil to give of its best.

THE PORTLAND ROSES

This group was also known as the damask perpetuals, because they came from crosses of the small group of recurrent-flowering damasks with other roses. They are themselves recurrent. In contrast to the damasks they make compact flower growth with short flower stalks. The first was produced in England *c* 1800 and named after the Duchess of Portland, who was an enthusiastic rose grower. In some intangible way this group has, up to now, always seemed to me to be of much importance. Indeed at one time *c* 1850, they were very popular and over 150 varieties were on offer. But they were overtaken by the hybrid perpetuals (Chapter 9). Even the Duchess herself, in the Portland Rose, has gone and all I can bring to very well deserved notice are the obtainable:

Comte de Chambord which, at 4ft × 3ft with good foliage, provides, intermittently, recurrent blooms of a rich pink fading to lilac on the edges of the petals. It is like Charles de Mills (page 65) in shape, but is less full. Comte de Chambord, 1820–83, represents one of the most charming facets of French characteristics. It is, as noted, an undated Portland Rose, but as a person he was a grandson of Charles X, and exiled in 1830. Only two nurserymen in the United Kingdom seem to stock it: and only one can provide the equally good:

Jacques Cartier who offers, to the same degree, clear pink flowers. They are carried on erect vigorous stems and are full, quartered and button-eyed. The name here is clearly indicated: it is that of the celebrated French navigator and explorer, 1494–1557, who followed Cabot in what has become the French part of Canada, especially as regards the gulf and river of St Lawrence.

CHAPTER 8

CENTIFOLIAS AND MOSS ROSES

It was long accepted that the centifolia rose of great fragrance, referred to by Theophrastus and Pliny (page 20) and so called by them, was the *Rosa centifolia* – the old cabbage rose – of the herbalists and our Victorian forebears and that it was the most ancient of roses.

Modern thought and research (the initial work being done by our much quoted Bunyard) is unable to accept that the ancient *R. centifolia* survived and is still with us. On the contrary, our *R. centifolia* has been with us from the eighteenth century only and it is not a wild species (whatever the ancient one may have been), but a complex hybrid evolved from four wild species – *R. rubra*, *R. phoenicia*, *R. canina* and *R. moschata* – and therefore of garden origin. The credit for this is given to Dutch breeders who worked from *c* 1580 to *c* 1700 to give us the beautiful original *R. centifolia*, whose progeny forms such an historical and enriching group.

Before we look at those members of the group which are still available, I would like to quote from what Thomas Rivers said about it 130 years ago, because this conveys to me and will, I think, do so to others, the quintessence of old roses. He writes:

> This rose has long and deservedly been the favourite ornament of English gardens ... it claims attention as much for its high antiquity as for its intrinsic beauty ... That 'Prince of gardeners', Millar, says that it is the prettiest of all roses; and this idea still prevails to a great extent in the agricultural districts of England, where, in farm and cottage gardens, the Cabbage Rose and the Double Wall-flower are most esteemed inmates; forming, in their turns, with a sprig of rosemary, the Sunday 'bouquet' of the respectable farm-servant and cottager.

It is all in Gray's *Elegy* too.

R. centifolia has various other names: Rose à Cent Feuilles (the Rose of a Hundred Leaves/Petals), the (Old) Cabbage Rose, *R. provincialis*, Provence Rose, Rose des Peintres. As to these I would like to make my own preliminary contribution by asking a question: has this rose in fact 100 petals and does a cabbage – if so, what variety – have 100 leaves? The answer to the first part is that I have never counted them, but nowhere in the books I have consulted does any writer *specifically* state that the petals total about 100. Perhaps it is regarded as obvious, or the 'hundred' is merely symbolic for 'an awful lot'. The second part is even more interesting in that some authorities take the view that 'cabbage' refers to 'shape' and not to 'leaves'; and, indeed, there is another view that the former is misapplied in that it more aptly describes roses in the hybrid perpetual class (Chapter 9). So be it: we gardeners must content ourselves with the consensus of opinion that *R. centifolia*, however named, and despite a once-flowering period only, is a very good garden rose with superlative, large, deep, button-centred, globular blooms with many clear pink petals and much fragrance. The heavy blooms have a great influence on the habit of growth, which gives 'open' and widespreading bushes with the very reasonable dimensions of 5ft × 4ft. These characteristics add up to a sturdy plant with 'a lax air', which can also be seen in its kindred:

— **bullata**, 1815, which is also called Rose à Feuilles de Laitue, the Monstrous or Cabbage-leafed Provence Rose. A sport of *R. centifolia* originating in Holland and a counterpart of its parent, except for height, 4ft, and foliage. The leaves are remarkably like those of the lettuce 'Continuity': large, bullate, hanging loosely and when young, tinted mahogany. Their effect is handsome and interesting, but they are inedible.

Fantin-Latour with its blush, flat, full-petalled prolific blooms, this is more than typical of the family as is the habit of growth, 6ft × 5ft. But the actual foliage, in its smoothness, is much like that of the China roses. However described, it adds up to a splendid garden rose with beautiful blooms. Fantin-Latour was, of course, the celebrated French painter, 1836–1904, whose name has so rightly been given to a rose.

Reine des Centfeuilles, 1824, although not so freely available, this is another pink of similar, very high qualities. Its flowers of clear pink reflex into a ball of lighter shade which is large, quartered and button-eyed and when fully open look as if the petals had been cut off quite flat. They come very freely. At 4ft × 3ft the plant is somewhat smaller than *R. centifolia*.

Chapeau de Napoléon, 1826, is the popular name of *R. centifolia cristata* or **Crested Moss**, but it is not a true moss rose because the moss is limited to the margin of the calyx and, as Bunyard adds: 'is an exaggerated development of the sepal margins'. But this unique feature does give quite a good reproduction of a cockaded three-cornered hat. *R. cristata* is a sport from *R. centifolia*, except that the blooms are perhaps not quite so globular, but they are quite as beautiful. The dimensions are similar: 5ft × 4ft. Unfortunately it can catch mildew and black spot too – mine seems to be immune.

We may as well continue with the other taller-growing varieties, but here is a convenient opportunity to make a point. People so often say that tall growers are not for small gardens. It seems to me that it is the width of the plant that matters. For example, *R. spinosissima* and most of its family rarely exceeds 3ft in height but its underground runners can be of almost limitless width (see also Belle Poitevine, page 54).

Tour de Malakoff, 1856, rated 6ft × 5ft, and accordingly demands some space, especially as the lax growth with the nodding grace and fullness of the blooms is typical of most centifolias. Those of Tour de Malakoff are, indeed, very large and peony-like. They vary in colour from cerise-magenta just on opening, go on to rich violet when full and finish grey-lavender. A redoubtable rose, a *tour de force*, but like some towers it may need buttressing.

La Noblesse, 1856, is perhaps less demanding at 5ft × 4ft, but it is entitled to more attention because it makes a compact bush and has better foliage than *R. centifolia*. Although the flowers are somewhat smaller, they have the characteristic shape, colour and fragrance and, very usefully, they come later than those of any other centifolia variety.

Variegata, 1845, has a wealth of popular names: **Village Maid, Cottage Maid, La Rubanée** and **Dometil Beccard**. It is a vigorous 5ft × 4ft, with large dark-leafed foliage. The globular flowers, coming singly and in clusters, are a beautiful creamy white striped in pale lilac-pink. They come freely, but are fleeting and dislike the rain: a pity – a comment which also applies to the fact that it may attract mildew.

Juno, 1847, although obtainable from only one nurseryman, has to be mentioned because it is in the 'superb bloom' class. The flowers are globular in shape, button-eyed in the midst of rolled, delicate blush petals and ultimately are quite flat. Lax growth put at 4ft × 4ft makes it suitable for hanging down from raised beds.

Robert le Diable is included for the same reason as Juno, also because it is a very late flowerer. The blooms resemble those of the gallicas and that variety could have had a hand in the production of the plant. Beautifully shaped, the flowers are of medium size, with outer reflexing petals. Against a prevailing parma violet they can produce petals of dark purple and intense cerise, while some are splashed with scarlet. The best colour range is obtained when the weather is hot and dry. The growth, 4ft × 3ft, is almost on the ground.

Petite de Hollande, also called **Petite Junon de Hollande, Pompon des Dames, Normandica,** is first-class as a garden plant. It is perfectly scaled down to a miniature *R. centifolia*, including the pink of the petals and, of course, the fragrance. The growth is compact and rather more bushy and so it is unarguably suitable for small gardens and popular (3–4ft × 3ft).

De Meaux, *R. centifolia pomponia* is another pink miniature, but as the Latin name shows, the flowers are 'pompon' in shape and formation and not miniature centifolias; but the foliage is, and of light green. Unfortunately, in some places it can suffer badly from black spot. Subject to this warning it makes a charming plant of much the same habit and dimensions as Petite de Hollande. Produced in the seventeenth century, it is named after Doménique Séguier, born 1637, and sometime Bishop of Meaux – so it has been guessed.

One can sum up the centifolias as a group having a high percentage of varieties with superlative flowers, but hardly of elegant growth, which is thorny, lax and open: this can mean support either by a wall or stakes, or by close planting. For most people who grow them the fragrant nodding blooms on arching stems far outweigh any disadvantages, to which some will add their need for a rich and well-fed soil for them to give of their best.

I am unable to produce very much about the number of centifolia varieties. In 1829 Desportes listed 120 centifolias and their hybrids: presumably that figure included the moss roses. Fifty years later Paul had nine centifolias in his catalogue. Here we have twelve (about twenty in 1964).

MOSS ROSES

The moss roses, which for many people epitomise all the 'old roses', take their place here because whatever the precise botanic status of the moss rose may be, one thing is certain: all authorities agree that the old 'Moss Rose and the old Cabbage Rose are closely allied'. The foregoing is a quote from Dr Hurst's *Notes on the Origin of the Moss Rose* which are reproduced in *The Old Shrub Roses* of Graham Thomas.

What is recorded there certainly epitomises all the work which the scientists and botanical systematists have put into the *genus rosa*.

The chief distinguishing characteristic between the moss rose and the centifolia group is, put quite simply, that the former have a moss-like growth on and around the sepals which in some cases is elongated and in most extends in more bristle-like form along the stems: technically, it is a bud-mutation (see page 147). Whether this characteristic and some others of a more detailed botanical kind justify a separate classification for the moss rose or is to be taken as only a variety of *R. centifolia*, seems to have exercised the minds to a greater or lesser extent of, according to Dr Hurst's *Notes*, no less than twenty-six systematists between 1760 and 1906.

Naturally, from what has been said on page 60 about the blurred divisions between groups, one is not surprised that moss roses show in some varieties not only the influence of the old cabbage rose, but also that of the damask rose and of the Chinas in their recurrency of blooms.

R. centifolia muscosa, the **Common Moss,** came to the UK from the Botanic Garden at Leyden, Holland in 1727 as a sport from *R. centifolia*. A single pink arose in 1807 and from that time other varieties were raised, but none of the pinks is considered to have greater beauty than that of the Common Moss. Its clear pink blooms are, as one might expect from what has been said above, in the early stage globular in shape; and when fully open they are flat, showing the button centre. They give off an exquisite fragrance. All the grace of the growth and foliage of *R. centifolia* is there too in its 4ft × 4ft, as well as the once-flowering period. The white form is equally beautiful:

Centifolia muscosa alba is its accepted full-dress name, but it is much more commonly called **Shailer's White Moss** and also **Bath, White Bath** or **Clifton Moss.** It seems to have been a sport, in 1788, from a Common Moss in the nursery of Henry Shailer in Chelsea. Shepherd says that the early plants were white, pale blush or striped (pink and white), but they were eventually segregated. The latter was put out in 1790 as the Striped Moss (but seems to have disappeared – at any rate commercially). In 1810, however, further white sports are said to have occurred in a garden at Clifton (presumably the 'Bristol' one) and in Bath. But Shepherd writes that the Bath/Clifton type was a purer white and more mossy than Shailer's, and that it superseded it. If the catalogues have the last word, they call it the White Bath, except one which offers Shailer's White Moss.

Anyway, despite slightly smaller flowers, and a limited liability to get mildew, its beauty equals that of its forebear, the Common Moss. Also, in my own experience, it is superior to the more than commonly available:

Blanche Moreau, 1880, which has the advantage of recurrent flowering (which is not all that forthcoming). Dark green foliage and dark brownish-green moss make a good foil for the creamy white flowers, which are not very shapely although very double and not all of one mind whether to be cupped or flat. With a height of 6ft and very lax growth it really does need support, and also sometimes needs protection against mildew.

Moreau presents a biographical problem. The rose is dated 1880. All I can offer for a choice is:
1 General Jean Victor, 1763–1813, a rival of Napoleon and who was killed fighting against the French in Russia.

2 Hégersiffe, a poet of 1810–38.

3 Gustave, an original and brilliant artist.

4 Moreau-Robert, the raiser, seems to be the answer.

We might now look at the pinks and begin with one which despite height does not need support, at any rate with me.

Comtesse de Murinais, 1843, which is noted for superlative blooms and vigorous growth, carries light green ribbed leaves up to 6ft. The green moss is hard to the touch. The flowers, when half open, are blush-white which fades to a milk-white to give well-formed, button-eyed flat blooms: they may be quilled or quartered. It is a pity that they are not recurrent.

Jeanne de Montfort, 1851, is certainly a very big girl, 7–8ft × 5ft whose growth is both bushy and vigorous, with leafy foliage and brown moss. The very mossy buds open to clear warm-pink flowers, which are loosely double and show effectively the yellow stamens. One can get some late blooms too. Obviously for the back of a border, or as a pillar rose. It does not get mildew with me but may do elsewhere.

James Mitchell, 1861, is undoubtedly a good and effective garden rose and worthy of wider distribution. It is usually the first moss to flower and does so along the length of strong stems, singly or in clusters. Each bloom is a perfect miniature, including a button eye, in magenta-pink which fades to soft lilac-pink and is well set off by browny-green moss, 5ft × 5ft.

Général Kléber, although not produced until 1856, commemorates the general whom Napoleon left to look after his army in Egypt. Nancy Steen says: 'He was a very kind man, much loved by his men.' On that character and from my experience, he deserves Graham Thomas's: 'In this variety, the pink mossy varieties reach their greatest perfection, apart from the Common Moss. It is the only Moss Rose I have seen which bears any resemblance to the clear and refined beauty of *Rosa alba* Celeste' (page 69). With respect, I agree. The double blooms open flat, show button eyes and are of outstanding quality. The foliage, 4–5ft × 4ft, is a fresh green and so is the ample moss.

Mousseline or **Alfred de Dalmas,** 1855, is a creamy blush-pink, found under either name in the catalogues. The blooms are cup-shaped with high centres and plenty of petals. They are somewhat small, but certainly recurrent, even to October, and they show that a damask rose was concerned in their origin. They are well shown off by dense foliage which is made up of spoon-shaped leaves – all making a compact bush about 4ft × 4ft. I am afraid that I do not know who Alfred de Dalmas might have been nor why the alternative name should be 'muslin'.

Gloire des Mousseux, 1852, in contrast to Mousseline's smallish blooms, has the distinction of giving what are claimed to be the largest flowers among the old garden roses, and very good they are too, their bright pink backed with clear green moss. When at their fullest they can reach 5in in diameter, and they show good quartering and button eyes. A sturdy plant – 4ft × 3ft – on which the light green foliage shows the blooms off well and they last quite a long time, during which the colour pales somewhat. An alternative name is **Mme Alboni.** Marietta Alboni was, it seems, a famous Italian opera singer who lived between 1824 and 1896.

There are three crimsons worth our attention:

Henri Martin, 1863, is in every aspect an elegant and dainty rose. The blooms are well shaped, with broad rounded petals neatly arranged. In colour they are the nearest to pure crimson in the moss group; it fades to a deep rose. The moss can hardly be described as copious, but it is adequate, in clear green. The foliage is that colour too. Henri Martin, as will have been noted, is dated 1863. There was a French impressionist artist of that name, born in 1860. There was also a celebrated French historian of the same name, whose dates are 1810–83. *Faites vos jeux, messieurs.*

Little Gem, 1880, is a uniform light crimson, and is included because, at about 2ft it is for the front of the bed or border, and is popular for that reason. The blooms are of the pompon type and are flat when fully open. The attractive foliage matches them in size. There is not very much moss.

Capitaine John Ingram, 1856, also carries flat pompon-type blooms but with button eyes; they are an intense purplish-crimson shaded with maroon, which changes to velvety soft tones of mottled purple. They come freely, but on the late side, and are not very mossy. The foliage is dark and neat. It makes a vigorous, bushy and splendid garden rose.

Nuits de Young, 1851, is another, even more popular, no doubt because of the distinctive habit, foliage and maroon-purple flowers. The latter are on the small side, showing golden stamens among the maroon-purple which is intense, dark and velvety. The foliage too is burnished with that colour and metallic tones, but the small and dark leaves come sparsely, so that the general effect of the 5ft × 3ft bush is wiry and slender. Altogether it may be described as very good but, personally, I would not put it in the same class as the Capitaine, and, in so deciding, I am not influenced by the fact that mildew warning may be necessary. But among the moss roses with outstandingly beautiful blooms I would put those of:

William Lobb, 1855, for their large, semi-double muddled centres and petals of dark crimson-purple with pale lilac-pink on the reverse side: twenty-four hours

Tour de Malakoff

later, the colour is lavender-grey. Truly the 'Old Velvet' Moss. The buds are much mossed and come in large clusters. The dark leaden-green foliage is on the small side for the plant's long stems which, although scheduled for 6ft, can often compete with Jeanne de Montfort by making 8ft, but unlike that variety it does need support either by growing in a group of its fellows or with other tall growers. One of mine is supported by a climbing Souvenir de la Malmaison (page 94) and it is said that it looks particularly well with the coral and salmon pink of the climber Albertine, no doubt because they will be able to enjoy mildew at the same time ...

Maréchal Davoust, 1853, yes, you are quite right, here is another Napoleonic officer, but the first marshal we have had. The rose is worthy of his rank. It has good foliage with pointed leaves and carries a plenitude of blooms, the buds of which have dark brown moss. On opening, the blooms show deep crimson-pink with a paler tone on the undersides; as they develop the petals are flushed with rich purple and lilac. This is topped off with button eyes and green pointels. At 4ft × 4ft – it is, by some rose measurements – little, but very good, on all counts.

Louis Gimard, 1877, has beautiful flowers too: they are lilac-crimson in the early stages, but when open there are various tones between lilac and crimson in their muddled centres. The foliage has rich green pointed leaves and the growth is 5ft × 3ft, but not so sturdy as the flowers are beautiful. Well worth having.

Salet

Deuil de Paul Fontaine, 1873, is so small, 3ft × 3ft, that despite very good and interesting blooms, seems to have dropped out of favour because a loss of vigour makes it no longer of great garden value. Nevertheless the buds and the large, cupped, globular flowers carry hard, reddish, prickly moss. The blooms show satiny mauve-crimson outside, while inside is a gamut of dark velvety tints: crimson, Tyrian rose, purple and maroon, cerise, to near black with brown shadings: quartered too. The stems are bristled and the leaves dark green.

Salet, 1854, is not all that wonderful, but is of convenient size, 4ft × 3ft, and is dependable in the recurrence of its clear pink blooms, which have narrow petals, are frequently quartered and have muddled centres. The foliage is soft light green. Can be summed up as 'useful'.

So far as one can ascertain the moss group as such was never very numerous: the largest number that I have seen quoted is 123 in France, and Rivers says in 1872, having discussed fifteen varieties: 'I have imported for several years every new Moss Rose raised in France, to the amount of nearly one hundred varieties, and have found but few worthy of cultivation.' Paul's catalogues do not seem to have exceeded 15 varieties. Here I have attained 18, ten years ago it would have been 32. More disturbing is that 5 have a warning about mildew. None of mine

---

FACING PAGE

Mme Isaac Pereire is magnificent in growth, with quartered blooms and raspberry fragrance

gets it, but I am assured by other people that it comes – *after* the flowers are over.

People who have had experience of them in the past would rate highly and lament the passing, or scant availability, of:

Duchesse de Verneuil, which I have in my garden and much admire the bright pink, button-eyed blooms, well set-off by bright green foliage;

Mme de la Roche-Lambert, a recurrent producer of crimson-purple blooms accompanied by fine moss;

Réné d'Anjou has soft pink muddled-centred blooms of grace and charm on a well poised bush.

Blanchefleur, with its hybrid-perpetual cabbage-type creamy white blooms of outstanding, but insufficiently recognised, beauty which comes from their multiplicity and rolled edges. The foliage, 5ft × 3ft, is somewhat coarse and the variety is related to:

Paul Ricault, of similar dimensions, habit and beauty save for the rich rose of its flowers.

If one likes beds, then the moss group could provide one of pretty near perfect balance in height and colour. In short: the Victorians had some good things and their moss roses were not among the least of them. The old roses are therefore secure in many hearts from their association and their beauty; how, it will be asked, do they stand today from the point of utility as garden plants?

———————————

FACING PAGE

(above left) Commandant Beaurepaire is striped in pink, purple, mauve and scarlet splashes. Has great fragrance
(above right) Reine des Violettes: this bourbonish purple is a bridge to the hybrid perpetuals. The quartered flattish blooms become a violet-grey or violet-purple
(below left) Souvenir du Dr Jamain and the (below right) Empereur du Maroc are typical hybrid perpetuals; the one 6ft × 3ft exhibits port wine and likes rich soil, the other 4ft × 3ft is vigorous in its deep velvety maroon. Both are rich in fragrance

CHAPTER 9

CHINAS, BOURBONS AND HYBRID PERPETUALS

These three groups are very closely related, although in different ways, and have one common and extremely important feature. They are all recurrent flowerers, albeit one or two varieties seem a bit doubtful as to whether they comprehend fully the meaning of 'recurrent' in this particular context.

CHINAS

I have been reading five different authors on these roses: of course, they are introduced in five different ways. But that of Graham Thomas's is so superior to the others and so much better than anything I could do, that I use it here:

> The China Rose is the foundation species upon which all our modern roses are built, whether they be bedding roses or shrubs or perpetual-flowering climbers. Its influence in rose-breeding over a hundred years has been so great, so overwhelming, and so potent that it is difficult to see where we should have been without it. We are so used to thinking of roses in terms of Hybrid Teas and Floribundas that we are apt to forget that these are, comparatively, very new and specialised, and they owe more than half their success and *éclat* to the China Rose.

I am persuaded that a simple story about the introduction of old roses to Europe or the UK is difficult to tell: that of the China rose is no exception. The books which I have been reading – identified by the year of publication – give me the following information:

1936: Baroness Oberkirch visiting Haarlem in 1782 and seeing the first China Rose growing there, recognised it at once (presumably from decorations on screens, fans etc).

First actual specimen of China rose seen in Europe was probably a dried specimen in the Herbarium of Gronovius now in British Museum.

The discovery of the wild species, however, was not made until Dr A. Henry, the great discoverer of Chinese plants, found it in a gorge at Ichang.

1954: Gronovius, the Dutch botanist is said to have received a dried specimen of the double blush form in 1704.

Planted in the Botanic Garden at Haarlem 1781 (Baroness Oberkirch must have seen the very first flowering period?).

That it had been brought to England at an earlier date and had been lost is not improbable.

However, no reliable records exist of its having reached England before 1789, when Sir Joseph Banks, then president of the Royal Society, brought it from Holland. The wild prototype, bearing single flowers ranging in colour from pink to red, was not discovered until 1885 ...

1955: Earliest records of the China rose are found in the Chinese screen paintings of the tenth century on which are portrayed Blush China Roses which appear to be identical with the Blush Tea-scented China introduced to England in 1809.

It may be this flower [the (wild) Pink China] which Montaigne saw at the Jesuit Monastery Ferrara in 1678 and was told that it flowered all the year round.

It seems that the Pink China was brought to Sweden by Peter Osbeck, a pupil of Linnaeus in 1752 and planted in the Botanic Garden at Uppsala, and was cultivated in England in 1759.

1973: With the Old Blush Peter Osbeck also sent to Uppsala *R. chinensis* × *odorata*, which arrived at Kew in 1769. Neither of these were used for breeding which came from later importations. G. Slater, a director of the East India Company introduced from Bengal, in 1792, a semi-double, crimson China rose *Rosa chinensis semperflorens*. It became known as Slater's Crimson China, but it was known in Britain through a herbarium specimen of Gronovius some sixty years earlier. The Old Blush China was reintroduced into England again from Bengal, by one Parsons, and it thus acquired the alternative name of Parsons' Pink China. Both the Crimson and the Pink, together with similar China roses, were cultivated varieties derived from the wild species *Rosa chinensis*, which incidentally is not available in Britain, and it was upon them that 'all our modern roses are built'.

Here I wish to identify the source of the information labelled '1973'. It comes from an article 'China Roses' in the *Rose Annual* of that year, by Tessa Allen, and the length of it is, if I may say so, some measure of its excellence.

Despite its youthfulness, and for the reason given on page 91, the illustration of Yesterday on page 104 gives no bad idea of what the near hybrids of *R. chinensis* look like.

After so much introductory matter, what I have to offer by way of available true China roses is an anticlimax. There are only five and even Slater's Crimson is not among them. They are:

Old Blush – Parsons' Pink China, Common Monthly, Old Pink Daily, Old Pink Monthly. The crimson-tinted buds open to a very soft pink which, in the common characteristic of the Chinas, deepens instead of fading as the blooms age. They come in large and small clusters. It will grow anywhere and, while it can make a 4ft hedge, unpruned in good soil against a warm wall it can reach 10ft. It is a rose without which no garden is complete.

Chinensis mutabilis, prior to 1896. Also called **Tipo Idéale** and sometimes, quite erroneously, *R. turkestanica*. A true Chinese rose and the most vigorous and perpetual. It is slender in growth, up to 8ft, with dark plum-coloured stems when they are young, while the foliage of that age is coppery. The flowers are single and have a long season: June to October. They are vivid orange and flame in the bud and open to a soft chamois yellow, but the flame continues on the underside. After being pollinated they change to a coppery pink, but before they fall this deepens (as one expects with the Chinas) to coppery crimson. This rose likes the sun and can stay in flower until Christmas.

Hermosa is sometimes classed as a Bourbon but Dr Hurst holds that it is a China-reversion. It is very like the Old Blush in habit, but seldom gets beyond 3ft × 3ft. Also, the blooms carry many more petals and give a round hep, whereas those of the Old Blush are oval: their colour is a gentle lilac-pink and they are fairly fragrant.

R. chinensis Mutabilis

Cramoisie Supérieure, 1832, also called **Agrippina**, gives us the deep crimson of **Slater's Crimson China,** which we cannot buy. It is a small bush, only 3ft × 2ft, with dark green small leaves. The double blooms come singly and in small clusters. As with its kindred, it esteems the sun.

R. chinensis viridiflora is the fifth and an odd one too, because it is correctly called the **Green Rose.** Flowering freely, it is a normal plant with similar growth to that of the Old Blush, but the petals and other parts of the flowers come as greenish scales. They make a charming, small, oval bud of soft blue-green. When, however, it opens this is lost and becomes loose and tawdry, splashed with brown. One suspects that it is bought as a curiosity: I did so buy it.

The foregoing is not a very exhilarating handful compared with the 252 varieties in Desportes's catalogue of 1832 nor, indeed, with William Paul's 170 in 1848 but, as hinted on page 88, we shall find the essential China rose in the recurrent flowering habit and the rich crimson of the bourbons and hybrid perpetuals, both of which do not have any lack of available varieties.

Before we go to them, however, there is a modern, 1973 rose which should be noticed. It is:

Yesterday which is described in the Royal National Rose Society's award of a Certificate of Merit as a floribunda-polyantha type from (Phyllis Bide × Shepherd's Delight) × Ballerina. This its raiser, Jack Harkness, has expanded, because on first seeing it I said it looked like a China rose:

> If Phyllis Bide is Perle d'Or × Gloire de Dijon, these are classed ... as a China and Noisette; Perle d'Or gets its China influence from its seed parent (an unnamed Polyantha), the class which is assumed to have started with a cross multiflora × *chinensis*. The other parent being a Tea ... Quite a mixture – if the records are to be trusted – but to my mind, Yesterday is more of a China than anything else.

A comparison of the illustrations on pages 90 and 104 is perhaps interesting.

As for its description: the bloom has a silvery base deepening to purple at the edges of the petals; semi-double, opening flat (1in diameter) with pronounced stamens, fragrant, borne in trusses. Small-leafed foliage in a glossy mid green, bushy and spreading.

The reason why I dealt with this very new variety rather fully will be clear from what is said in Chapter 13.

Also, there are some items of miscellanea which should be disposed of.

There is a small class of nineteenth-century roses called polypompons, which became popularly known as polyanthas (subsequently to be called floribundas). *R. chinensis minima* is said to have been a parent, but *R. multiflora* looms much more largely – even if not then, certainly in the subsequent developments of a hybrid which in the second generation produced the two original polypompons.

In turn one of them was much crossed with other varieties including the tea roses. In the result – quite unjustifiably botanically, but said to be justified horticulturally – certainly three outstandingly good and very popular roses, having apparently no trace of the China rose in their make-up, are included under that heading in catalogues and even by writers. For that reason they are mentioned briefly here:

Cécile Brunner, 1881, a 'dainty tea-polyantha', 3ft × 2ft, is an exquisite miniature with thimble-sized pale pink hybrid tea-type blooms. It is very recurrent, but needs good soil and the sun. The climbing form, with slightly larger flowers, can in those conditions reach 20ft.

Bloomfield Abundance, briefly, is a very much larger, 8ft × 8ft, 1920 edition of Cécile Brunner. The yellow **Perle d'Or**, 1883, 4ft × 3ft, is like Cécile too and has almost as much beauty and recurrency of bloom.

BOURBONS

These are said to have originated from a cross between Quatre Saisons (the pink Autumn Damask, *R. damascena bifera*, page 71) and Parsons' Pink China (? Old Blush, page 90).

The one certain fact about this family is that it reached France from the then Ile de Bourbon (later, Ile de la Réunion) in the Indian Ocean in 1819. It arrived in England in 1822 and in the USA in 1828. A hybrid, it was in that year named *R. bordoniana*, by Narcisse Desportes. One parent was clearly *R. chinensis* – Parsons' Pink China – and the more certain view seems to be that the other was one of Pliny's twelve Roman roses, namely *R. damascena bifera*, the Autumn Damask

Boule de Neige

(see page 71). Locally, and in the neighbouring Mauritius, it was called **Rose Edward.**

Dr Hurst points out that it was in the seeds which the curator of the Botanical Gardens in the Ile de Bourbon, Bréon, sent in 1819 to France. They were received in Paris by Jacques, the gardener to King Louis-Philippe, who from them raised the first French Bourbon, giving it the name **Rosier de l'Ile Bourbon.** Semi-double in form, a brilliant rose in colour, and of great fragrance, especially in the abundant blooms of the autumn. For good measure the foliage was nearly evergreen, of compact and vigorous growth with glossy largish leaves.

Thereafter, this, the bourbon rose, provided the hybridists with a new and welcome field for their work, and there was no holding them; the results certainly retained the charm of the old garden roses. The available remains of this work are

Souvenir de La Malmaison

given here: practically all the varieties are judged to have either superlative blooms or are recommended for general effect and garden value; seven achieve both. They are recurrent, except where otherwise noted, and are set out here in colour groups, which marry well with the old roses and, indeed, with the modern hybrid teas, although they are somewhat coarser. Moreover, they cover the whole colour range – white, flesh, pink, mauve and maroon, but no yellows. Some can grow to great heights.

Boule de Neige, 1867. When fully open the flowers are perfect in outline, in colour of ivory white, in the camellia-like arrangement of the petals and in 'sweetness of fragrance'. The growth is erect, 6ft × 4ft and the foliage is dark green. It is in great demand and, taken in conjunction with the similar situation

93

which the hybrid perpetual **Frau Karl Druschki** occupies, it seems to me to underline our lack of a really good white hybrid tea. But, like the Frau, it can, it is said, get black spot, although I have never seen it on my two bushes.

Souvenir de la Malmaison is not only the senior by age (1843) of the recurrent varieties, but gives ceaselessly wonderful, soft, creamy-blush blooms, quite flat, much quartered and of a delicate fragrance – some people say that its full excellence is not attained until the second crop. It is an excellent plant with good foliage on strong stems; 4ft × 3ft. There is a climbing form, 10ft × 8ft, with somewhat larger flowers, but less of them in the autumn flush.

Souvenir de St Anne's has to be mentioned here because the only parent was Souvenir de la Malmaison, which created this nearly single sport when it was apparently over 100 years old, in its own image except for the nearly single flowers, which are nevertheless outstanding in their own way. It has a beautiful, sculptured shape with delicate tints of pink outside, and inside, white-blush. Its fragrance is stronger too. The plant gradually builds up to 6ft × 4ft.

Mme Pierre Oger, 1878, is a sport from La Reine Victoria with which it is identical in everything but colour. This is a warm creamy blush on opening and remains so in dull weather, but when the sun is out the petals change to clear rose which becomes intense if the sunshine is really hot. Like those of **La Reine**, the petals are unique in their shell-like beauty and dainty perfection. Apparently a popular rose but certainly needs protection in some areas against disease, as indeed does her mother:

La Reine Victoria, 1872, who basks in the fame of its relative but equally merits

Madame Pierre Oger

94

La Reine Victoria

fame on its own account. Each is tall and slender, 6ft × 3ft, from a continual supply of fresh shoots which have narrow smooth leaves and carry exquisite, full and circular cup-shaped flowers of delicious fragrance. The flowers of La Reine are an intense rose-madder or, if one prefers, 'old rose', which in the centre and at the base of the petals is much paler.

Louise Odier, 1851, completes a trio of roses renowned for the exquisite shape of their flowers. Here the colour is a warm pink shaded with lilac. The blooms come almost continuously and are full, cupped, circular and deliciously fragrant. The growth is vigorous and the foliage is a rich fresh green; 6ft × 4ft.

Mme Lauriol de Barny, 1868, is not so well known as the trio, no doubt because it gives only one and an early flush of its large, double, beautiful flowers of light silvery pink. The fragrance is said to be fruity. There may be the odd bloom or so later on. The blooms are carried along arching stems with sparsely furnished smooth leaves. Grown as an open bush it reaches 5ft; as a pillar rose it can make 6–7ft.

Kathleen Harrop is a late arrival, 1919, compared with Zéphirine Drouhin's 1868, from which it sported to give a 7ft × 5ft plant with a constant supply of pretty flowers in clear pink with a light crimson reverse. Otherwise it is like its parent, especially in its raspberry fragrance.

Adam Messerich seems almost made for Kathleen Harrop: only a year younger, with raspberry fragrance, and similar dimensions. It makes a fine upstanding bush with stout nearly thornless green wood, and produces semi-double cupped flowers in a heavy summer crop. Both varieties are very good in the garden. No diffi-culties of consanguinity and so on should arise. Kathleen had no father; Adam was a mixture of a HT – Frau Oberhofgärtner-Singer – crossed with a hybrid from a Louise Odier seedling and a centifolia, Louis-Philippe. People being what they are, most of them ignore the wife of the garden foreman and concentrate on the aristocratic Bourbon, which is why the former is included here.

Mme Ernst Calvat, 1888, has unique crimson-purple foliage on its young lusty stems. At 7ft × 5ft it is a vigorous pillar rose, but it can be kept pruned to make an excellent open shrub with the foliage acting as a foil to very large, globular, cabbage-like but superlative blooms in clear pink with darker reverses to the petals. The raspberry fragrance is very strong this time. May get mildew but not from her only parent:

Mme Isaac Pereire, 1880, who is another winner with powerful growth at 6–8ft × 5ft. Has handsome foliage measuring up to the enormous flowers, which are a light madder-crimson on rolled petals, quartered and opening to a breakfast-saucer face. The early blooms may be sometimes a little misshapen, but thereafter they are uniformly handsome. I have grown it as a lusty shrub: now a new one at the end of the second year on a fence is over halfway to its ultimate 15ft. I have always regarded it as the most strongly scented rose in my garden and have been prepared to go along wholeheartedly with the description of it as 'one of the really great old roses of the nineteenth century', but for the fact that in 1973 it produced, for the first time, black spot in the early leaves. Rich raspberry fragrance. Her seedling, Mrs Paul, is similar but the colour is blush.

Prince Charles. Despite the fact that this is sold by one nurseryman only, I am including it here as a good garden rose which ought not to be lost to commercial growing. It does not flower a second time. The blooms have a flat, crimped, veined appearance and are a light madder-crimson, which becomes flushed with maroon-lilac; these colours become accentuated by the almost white centre. The leaves are smooth lead-green and are a good foil to the blooms. The Prince is in my garden.

Reine des Violettes, 1860, is usually found under the hybrid perpetuals, but Graham Thomas says that it can very well be grouped with the bourbons, as it so nearly approaches them in all characters. With respect, I agree from my own experience and continue to quote from him:

> This sumptuous variety needs a good soil to develop its colour and fairly hard pruning every February alone will enable it to produce its best. Its best is so good that no purplish-coloured rose can compare with its wide, flat blooms, quartered and with button eye in the old tradition; in dull weather they open to cerise-red ... but

quickly develop the soft violet-grey or lilac-purple which is unsurpassed by 'old' or the new 'blue' roses. Fortunately the foliage is ample and has a greyish tinge, just what is needed.

To this I add that it has excellent fragrance, grows to 6ft × 5ft and can be used as a shrub, or pegged down, or on a wall.

Zéphirine Drouhin, 1868, can be a 15ft climber or it may be kept pruned down to a bush. I have grown it many years in its natural way and there are two so treated in my garden now: one has managed 10ft and the other 8ft. It must be me. The flowers are loosely double and bright carmine-pink, sweetly scented – raspberries – and the leaves are coppery-purple when young and light green on maturity. To keep each other company in the intensive care ward against mildew, I am adding another bourbon climber:

Blairii Number Two was raised in 1845 with **Blairii Number One**, which was not very good and certainly not in commercial growing, even if it still exists. **Number Two,** however, is an outstandingly good and vigorous plant ultimately reaching to 25ft on wall or pillar. The long arching shoots carry mahogany-tinted foliage and very large blooms. These are fully double and have rich pink in the centre, while the outer petals are somewhat paler. When fully open they are veined and without doubt of unique beauty, especially when grown, for support, among other shrubs. There is only one source of supply, but even with the limitation of flowering only once, they ought to be more freely available.

We finish with four striped varieties and work from front to back:

Ferdinand Pichard

Ferdinand Pichard, 1921, is another new arrival in the UK from California, and the smallest – 4ft × 3ft – but one of the best, with fully globular flowers having outstandingly good stripes of crimson and crimson-purple on a pink ground, and of rich fragrance. The foliage has pointed leaves of yellowish green. This and other features point to a connection with:

Commandant Beaurepaire, 1874, which produces only a few flowers after a spectacular first flush. The flowers are round, cupped, incurved and fairly full. On a background of light carmine-pink are striped and splashed rose-madder, carmine, purple and, inside, an occasional slash of blazing scarlet. They are very fragrant too. The leaves are a curious light yellowish-green, long-pointed and of undulating formation. Also known as **Panachée d'Angers**, its dimensions are 5ft × 5ft and altogether it makes an elegant and effective garden rose. I like to think that this name refers to Nicolas-Joseph, a French officer, defending Verdun against the Prussians who killed himself rather than face the surrender of that fortress. My generation will note that Verdun was in French history long before 1916. It is said to have a sport in:

Honorine de Brabant which is equally effective, if not more so, as it is seldom out of flower. It is larger and perhaps coarser: it is certainly lusty, 8ft × 9ft, with much large leathery foliage, mid green in colour. The blooms are very pale lilac-pink, striped and spotted with darker tones, which vary from mauve to violet. The later flowers are particularly good. She and the Commandant are deservedly popular.

Variegata di Bologna, 1909, is tall, 8ft on good soil, with good shoots and so needing support of some kind. The blooms are another 'spectacular' with their dark crimson-purple stripes on a white ground. They are of good shape too – globular, well filled, quartered and well distributed along the arching stems, which carry narrow pointed foliage. But, and it is a big one, if there is a trace of black spot or other disease in one's garden, then the odds are well on that Variegata di Bologna will surely get it, with the twenty gold-beater force like that of the arm of the law which came down on Mr Pickwick and his friends at Ipswich. A great pity.

Gruss an Teplitz, 1897, is of such mixed parentage that no one seems to know into what family it should go. However, as there is something of the Bourbon in its blood and horticulturally, a place is found here as a tailpiece. But there is clearly a deal of China about it too, as shown by the small clusters of cupped dark crimson flowers which hot sunshine can intensify. They come continuously and the later shoots, 6ft or even more, may carry twelve or more blooms: these have a raspberry fragrance to some people, to others it is spicy. The foliage is light green, after being purple in youth.

I am sorry not to be able to finish, as usual, by giving the number of Bourbon varieties in Desportes's catalogues, but Shepherd writes: 'European catalogues listed them in unbelievably large numbers, and in America the 1846 catalogue of the Prince Nursery listed 144 varieties … '. Paul in 1864 offered 61. I have been able to produce only 19.

HYBRID PERPETUALS

It is hardly surprising, seeing what has gone before them, that the hybrid perpetuals have a very complex ancestry, and that their characteristics are reflected in the many different varieties which the group includes.

As the dates show, the bourbons and the hybrid perpetuals came about at much the same time – the former being somewhat earlier – and they developed in parallel for many years: no doubt, there was some interbreeding and their own special features became merged. For instance, the bourbon **Mme Isaac Pereire** and her sport, **Mme Ernst Calvat**, are very near to being hybrid perpetuals.

The bourbons retained, in the main, 'the charm of the old roses', but, hybrid perpetuals were not so successful in that way and can now be described as rather coarse hybrid teas. Nevertheless, out of their thousands of varieties – said to be 3,000 – and about fifty years of rocket-like popularity, they produced some quite good roses. Those still available and in my opinion worth while, are given below in order of seniority.

Général Jacqueminot, 1853. No, not one of Napoleon's. I have seen this rose described in one line: 'A famous rose of bright crimson; well-filled flowers. Excellent fragrance.' I have read its story in a 500-word article under his name, 'A Worthy Warrior', and from this I quote:

> To its other many virtues Général Jacqueminot was to add what to the rose breeder is the cardinal virtue – the ability to transmit its good characteristics, both as a prolific pollinator and seed parent. So successful was it in this rôle, that there are more than 520 recorded roses directly descended from it and, in addition, there are probably dozens or even hundreds of other unrecorded crosses in which it figured. In fact almost all of the great crimson hybrid perpetuals of the Victorian era were offspring of this truly great rose …
>
> The part played by Général Jacqueminot in his country's history was of minor importance and of short duration and although the general won a degree of renown on the battlefield, he achieved real fame in the rose gardens of the world.

On this evidence, that total of 3,000 given above must be about right. These celebrated flowers are fully double, large and cabbagey, very fragrant, free blooming and free growing on good stems, which sometimes take it to 6ft, and with good fresh green foliage. By today's standards it is outclassed. Also called **La Brillante, Richard Smith, Triomphe d'Amiens, Mrs Cleveland, General**

Jack, Jack Rose, but not the avuncular Cobleigh! Sometimes fails to defend himself against mildew.

Empereur du Maroc, 1858, has the normal dimensions of the Général, 4ft × 3ft; the foliage is small and sparse, but actually it is quite vigorous and produces flowers freely. They are an intense, dark carmine with a velvety maroon flush and are unique among the bourbons, the Chinas and their own kind. Splendid fragrance.

Prince Camille de Rohan, 1861, has flowers, according to Rivers, 'very double – not large – and its petals slightly reflexed. It forms a pillar rose of much beauty – its flowers are so rich and deep in their colouring.' The last statement is very true as they are dark velvety maroon, shaded at the petal edges with blood red, but it omits to say that their stems are weak. Habit makes it a splendid leafy bush but, at 4ft, hardly for a pillar. The Général is behind him and has also passed on the proclivity for additional names, which are: **La Rosière, Souvenir d'Auguste Rivoire** and **Edouard Dufour**. Like those of the Général, his defences against disease can sometimes break down.

Souvenir d'Alphonse Lavallée, 1884, is another beauty, of minimal availability. The very double sweetly fragrant blooms are beautifully shaped although small, but the colour, especially when the flowers are half open, is remarkable: intense, velvety, dark maroon-crimson with near black shading, no hint of purple. A tall (7ft × 4ft) sparse grower with foliage of small mid green leaves. It likes good soil and, when grown pegged down, it is smashing.

Souvenir du Dr Jamain

Souvenir du Docteur Jamain, 1865, is said to need special attention to its siting. It should be away from the sun, say, facing west. Good soil is essential and, I would add, fertiliser. The trouble is that the petals burn and go brown in hot sun. This is a pity as the blooms are beautiful, both by association and in themselves: they are a velvety, rich, port wine colour clouded over with maroon-purple. It is very fragrant and gives another lot of flowers in September. The Général is here again, and so is a warning about mildew.

Gloire de Ducher, 1865. With dimensions of 7ft × 5ft it is suitable as a pillar or on a wall; at any rate it should be supported. There is, however, another alternative in connection with other tall growers, 'pegging down' which is dealt with on page 146. The blooms are of fine quality in dark velvety crimson-purple with maroon shadings; some petals are quilled and folded. The foliage is some-what loose growing, with dark green leaves. Another feature is that the top ends of the new growth produce even larger blooms than those of the first crop.

Baroness Rothschild, 1868, also **Baronne Aldolphe de Rothschild,** is included in the list because it intrigues me. Apart from the rose *vade mecum*, *Modern Roses*, this variety seems to be mentioned by only one author among those I have consulted, yet it is offered by no less than seven nurserymen. According to Nancy Steen, who had difficulty in finding it in New Zealand, it is mentioned in *Roses for English Gardens* (1902) by Jekyll and Mawley. Mrs Steen records 'compact upright growth, stiff, short-jointed, green stems, and full of foliage around the shapely, non-fragrant, shallow, cup-shaped blooms of a clear rose-pink. These flowers generally appear singly and are held quite erect.' And a nurseryman's catalogue says: 'Exquisite shell-pink to rose. Very large and very double flowers, a robust grower'; he gives it a 'medium scented' marking. It is a pity that her sport, **Mabel Morrison,** whose blooms of palest pink going to flesh-white also rank as exquisite, is no longer available.

Paul Neyron, 1869, is still grown for its enormous cabbage-like blooms in deep rosy pink, and now, for a reason which will appear, I am going to continue from Graham Thomas: 'Rather like Peace in size and shape, but flatter, sometimes quartered and more filled with petals … Of no special ornament in the garden, and of no attraction to the nose, but a luxury to cut.' Paul is in my garden and I entirely agree, especially as I am no admirer of Peace. Incidentally, the growth and foliage are somewhat similar: of Paul Neyron's it is said: 'An extra vigorous plant up to 6ft with copious, large, glossy foliage in mid-green.'

Baronne Prévost, 1842, is a famous rose, at any rate in the USA, but now only available at one nursery in the UK. In 1848, however, William Paul's catalogue was saying: 'Flowers clear, pale rose, glossy, very large and full; form compact. Habit erect; growth robust. A superb kind. Raised by M Desprez of Yèbles.

Mrs John Laing

One of the largest.' To this he could have added that the blooms were flat, button-eyed, quartered, fragrant and the compactness measured 5ft × 3ft. It is well worth having in one's garden.

Ulrich Brunner Fils, 1882, is not in the superlative class, as I know from my own experience, but people buy it and it is certainly not a bad rose nor one to be despised, even though the flowers have been described as rather vulgar. They are bright cerise-red or, if preferred, rosy-red to vivid lilac-pink: it is like **Mrs John Laing** in growth, with good foliage and 6ft × 4ft dimensions.

Mrs John Laing, 1887. Although, unlike Graham Thomas, I cannot claim to be 'one who was brought up smelling this rose – and even complaining of its ubiquity in a small garden', I do claim it (and I have one only) as a very dear friend of over ten years' standing and one which, amid a plethora of pinks, gives me the most

Roger Lambelin

aesthetic appreciation. Indeed as one who regards Dean Hole, *lèse-majesté*, as something of a bore, it is a pleasure to go with his: 'Not only in vigour, constancy, and abundance, but in form and features, Beauty's Queen.' No other rose has such a delightful tone of soft pink with a faint lilac blush. It is full, very fragrant and complemented by perfectly fitting bright green foliage. The vigour can take it to 6ft, but I would put it at 5ft × 3ft. The light for mildew is amber.

Roger Lambelin, 1890, a sport from **Prince Camille de Rohan**, with the same weak stems, is famous for its 'different' blooms. Of excellent fragrance, they are, when at their best, a beautiful crimson-purple, deckle-edged with white, but when the crimson-purple fades goes to maroon-crimson. To be at its all-round best this variety needs good rich loam and, in my experience, rich feeding too.

FACING PAGE

(above left) Golden Chersonese (1970) E. F. Allen (*R. ecae* × Canary Bird)
(above right) Yesterday (1972) Jack Harkness (*R. chinensis* blood from [Phyllis Bide × Shepherd's Delight] × Ballerina)
(below left) News (1968) E. B. Le Grice (Lilac Charm × Tuscany Superb)
(below right) Picasso (1971)   Sam McGredy   (Marlena × [Evelyn Fison × (Orange Sweetheart × Frühlingsmorgen)])

G

It may not always stunt itself to death, but it needs to fight against disease. Mine did die, so I am with those who much prefer something less bizarre but more certain. This is:

Baron Giraud de l'Ain, 1897, less famous than Roger Lambelin it has its own claims to be noticed. The large flowers have full crimson petals and the edges are irregularly white, rather than deckled. Moreover, the outer petals are reflexed to give the shape of a saucer, while those in the centre stay as they are and give that of a cup. It is truly a striking bloom with a rich fragrance. The flowers are produced freely in summer, less so later, on a sturdy vigorous bush with broad rounded leaves.

Vick's Caprice, 1897, is included because of its useful size, 3ft × 2ft, its striped shapely blooms (like those of Mrs John Laing) and also, four nurserymen over here think it worth offering. The blooms come freely and are 'old rose', pink splashed and striped white, very fragrant too. The foliage is quite acceptable. It sported from a rose called Archiduchesse Elisabeth d'Autriche in a garden at Rochester, NY, United States. The owner's name is obvious.

Although I have reckoned – at any rate in my own mind – that the limit of my field is the end of the nineteenth century, it would be pedantic to draw a rigid line, especially if, in so doing, worthwhile rose varieties were excluded. Accordingly we will venture into the twentieth century to the extent of ten years.

Frau Karl Druschki, 1901, is an old friend of mine, as I have always produced her as that 'Scentless Cold White Wonder' when rebutting complaints that the

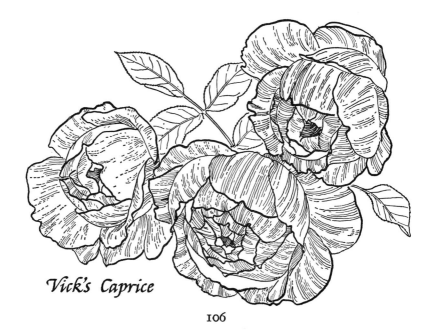

Vick's Caprice

hybridists have bred out in the modern roses the beautiful fragrance of the old garden varieties. To the joy of my perverted sense of humour I record that I have just discovered that Graham Thomas through his customary pedigree research has established, certainly to his satisfaction and therefore to mine, that it is not a hybrid perpetual but a hybrid tea. But, as Graham Thomas adds, in general appearance it certainly conforms fairly well to the hybrid perpetuals: certainly so in its light green foliage and in the vigour and erectness of growth, which with me is never less than 6ft, and means that it gives many more flowers if it is pegged down. It is readily available, which is not surprising as its hybrid tea type flowers have not been surpassed by those of any later white hybrid tea.

It is also known as **Reine des Neiges, Snow Queen,** and **White American Beauty**, any one of which names most people would regard as more descriptively suitable than that of the wife of the then president of the German Rose Society. However, by quite undeservedly failing to win in 1900 a competition for the best unnamed seedling of German origin, this chaste white beauty escaped the compulsory condition of being named Otto von Bismark.

A rose much like the Frau in habit and petal formation is:

Hugh Dickson, 1905, whose classification as a hybrid perpetual has so far not been challenged and time does not allow me to continue the very elementary research I have begun: nor does it matter. At sixty-nine years he remains a very vigorous old favourite who long held pride of place among the scarlet-crimson roses of hybrid tea type, large and full. The vigour of the growth is almost a handicap, as it easily reaches 10ft before flowering. The answer is to peg it down or train it along a fence or low wall. The foliage is as handsome as the flowers, but as with Frau Karl Druschki, there is a warning about mildew: in my garden in twelve years it has appeared on neither. There is a **George Dickson**, with modest growth, nodding dark crimson blooms and, by all report, no modesty about its mildew. I have not touched it. Unlike the Frau, Hugh Dickson is very fragrant.

Georg Arends, 1910, is the last variety to be mentioned under the heading of 'Old Garden Roses' and, fittingly enough, it is the last that ought to be mentioned, because without a shadow of doubt it is a hybrid tea and not a hybrid perpetual. How could it be otherwise with Frau Karl Druschki as one parent and the first hybrid tea, **La France** (1867), as the other? But I am not going to let that stop me here, because it is an outstandingly beautiful rose and of great garden value. Graham Thomas says in *Shrub Roses of Today* (1962), 'I cannot improve on the description in my *Manual of Shrub Roses*.' The very much less so can I. Here it is:

No other pink rose raised before or since has flowers of similar beauty; each petal rolls back in a beautiful way, and the flower, from the scrolled bud to the blown bloom, retains its clear, strawberry-ice pink; the cream is mixed in the reverse of the petals – 'Druschki' growth and foliage. Delicious scent.

What a pity it does not qualify, even under 'Old Garden Roses', for inclusion in the *Selected List of Varieties* of the Royal National Rose Society.

As to the numbers which were available in this group – leaving aside a figure of 3,000 which I have seen somewhere – one finds William Paul, in the 1884 edition of his catalogue, listing over 800. This was probably their apogee of popularity, but they went on until the end of the century, by which time the hybrid teas had established their ascendancy. Ninety years later there are only fourteen true HPs available to gardeners in the British Isles.

TEA ROSES

'Tea Roses' have been mentioned. They are within the classification 'Old Garden Roses', but they are not included in this book because they do not do at all well in the climate of Britain, no doubt because they need a garden sheltered from spring frosts and biting winds: a glasshouse, not a garden, rose. Moreover, so far as I know, they are obtainable from one nurseryman only. Despite this an outstandingly good and beautiful climbing tea is described on page 115.

Here we finish with the varieties in the old garden roses. A short summary may be permitted. Together with the wild roses and Climbers they total *c* 250, which compared with the 10,953 covered by the 1906 *Nomenclature de tous les Noms de Roses connus*. They must have served our gardening ancestors well for even that small number to have survived commercially in the British Isles, but one cannot be other than much impressed by the high proportion which bear French names. The encouragement which the Empress Josephine gave to the hybridists of that country through her collection at Malmaison was noted in Chapter 1, but my friend Mrs Gore in her Preface (page vi) came up with a most interesting explanation of the dominance of the French. It is:

The real source of the eminence of the French in the culture of roses, is the fact that it absorbs the almost exclusive attention of their horticulturists. The high price of fuel places the cultivation of the tender exotics (by which English amateurs are chiefly engrossed) almost out of the question; and as the French adhere to the wise custom of repairing to their country seats in May, and quitting them in December, their attention and money are appropriated to the improvement of such plants as adorn the flower-garden during the summer season. They care little for any that cannot be brought to perfection in the open air; and precisely the same motive which promotes the cultivation of the dahlia in England, has brought the rose to greater perfection in France.

We may well take this opportunity to look at the warnings about certain varieties being susceptible to disease in some areas. The wild roses are minimal, not more than $1\frac{3}{4}$ per cent. Among the old garden roses we find some 7 per cent may get black spot alone or, as regards most of them, that disease combined with mildew or rust, while 13 per cent may be assailed by mildew.

CHAPTER 10

CLIMBERS

There are old climbers and wild species roses whose natural state is to climb or ramble. Most of them are not well known either for themselves or in their hybrids. Moreover, many are to be found at only one source of supply. As to this I have adopted the same test for inclusion as applied to the wild and old garden roses (see page 17), that is, there should be more than one nurseryman in Britain making a variety available, unless quality in all respects makes it a really desirable garden rose or it is of such general interest that its preservation ought to be encouraged.

The varieties follow hereafter on the same principle as that adopted for the wild roses in Chapter 2, that is, the wild species (and here, or horticultural groups) are followed by their sports and hybrids, whether created by themselves or by man.

It is fitting that, alphabetically, one has to begin with:

R. arvensis because it is a wild native climber in the British Isles and to a lesser extent in most of Europe. Known also as the Field Rose it is a rampant grower climbing through waste land, thickets, hedges and up trees, and unchecked can form dense mounds of slender stems. It has – to quote the catalogue of the only nurseryman who can supply it – 'leaves with five to seven shining green leaflets persisting late into winter. Flowers, 4 to 5cm across, white with little or no fragrance, appearing in July; fruits rounded or oval, dark red.' Not all that thrilling, but I am adding it to my collection because my own researches have given me so much interest. Shepherd has suggested that:

It may quite possibly be the Musk Rose of Shakespeare as well as the white rose that was chosen as an emblem of the House of York during the Wars of the Roses. At one time, *R. arvensis* was referred to as the English Musk Rose, as the fragrance of the blossoms is slightly reminiscent of musk. Several references to the Musk Rose in Shakespeare's *Midsummer Night's Dream* may apply to *R. arvensis*.

He goes on to say that the writer of an article in the 1931 *Rose Annual* of the Royal National Rose Society states:

that he had visited Towton, in Yorkshire, many times and that he had found several wild roses growing there. Towton was the scene of the battle in which Edward IV led the Yorkists to a decisive victory over the Lancastrians. His descriptions of the roses native there surely do not apply to *R. alba*, the rose that has long been presumed to have been the one that was chosen by the House of York as its insignia. The area is described as having many wild roses that bear single creamy white blossoms and whose low branches, with abundant thorns, often form impassable thickets. This description applies to *R. arvensis* and it is quite possible that a rose which was native and very common in Yorkshire was chosen as the emblem by the Yorkists. Writers have stated repeatedly and without reservations that *R. alba* was the species, but there is a distinct possibility that they may have been wrong.

Considering the number of wild roses which have come to us from East Asia and China, it is hardly surprising that a large number of climbers have to be included under the umbrella of China.

CHINA

Alphabetically one begins with the Boursaults. In my early interest in, and almost complete ignorance of, the old roses, these made by their very name quite an impression on me: they sounded terribly important and top-drawerish. Unfortunately, they were extremely few in number at their zenith and have now nearly disappeared. The original Boursault – *R. lhertierana* or *R. boursaultii* produced prior to 1820 – was long supposed to be a cross, *R. chinensis* × *R. pendulina*, until Mr Gordon Rowley pointed out that the marriage would not work. But so far neither he nor anyone else has been able to name a substitute for *R. pendulina*. All that Shepherd (1954) says about the group is based on *R. pendulina* and he implies that the number of varieties once known was approximately fifty. He names eight. However, Paul's catalogue for 1876–7 includes only two varieties, which by 1898 had risen to four. As of now, we have available:

Amadis, 1829, the **Crimson Boursault**, a crimson-purple, has fully double flowers in clusters, which come recurrently from early June. The thornless stems, with smooth foliage, can make up to 16ft. It is a spectacular climber and a good garden rose. That it has lasted for over 140 years is confirmation. The name is that of Amadis de Gaulle, surnamed Chevalier au Lion, the hero of a Portuguese-Spanish romance (1508) translated into French.

Mme de Sancy de Parabère, 1874, only just gets in here because it was no longer available, but one nurseryman in Britain now has it again. This news came from E. F. Allen, who most kindly followed it by sending me one from his own garden. By the time this is read I shall know all about it at first hand. In the meantime, its soft pink bloom is said to be one of the largest of all climbers – about 5in in diameter. Usually the outer petals are much larger and make a saucer surrounding a cup of short petals in the centre. The blooms come out all along arching stems. Like Amadis, it makes a spectacular but scentless plant and goes up or along to 15ft.

It may be recollected that for convenience I included the only bourbon climber – Blairii Number Two – in the bourbons on page 97. This is evened up here by including the only boursault bush rose:

Morlettii, 1883, takes its name from the raiser Morlet, and gives good value from spring to autumn. The blooms come early in clusters of small to medium-sized double flowers in magenta. Their display is not repeated. But it is more than completed by the arching 5ft × 5ft foliage, which in spring is richly red-tinted and becomes greyish-green with reddish veins and stalks. Throughout the autumn the colour is a brilliant orange and red. It has little or no scent. I have included it, because it is also little known and very worthy of being available at more than one nursery.

R. banksiae albo-plena, 1807, the **Banksian Rose**, Lady Banks's Rose (named after the wife of Sir Joseph Banks, who is justly regarded as one of the best ever directors of the Royal Botanic Gardens, Kew). The small, double, rosette-like white flowers are carried on slender almost thornless shoots which can reach 25ft. It has to mature before giving blooms in great abundance and only then, which is in May and June, when on a warm wall in full sun. As the flowers, with the fragrance of violets, come on the previous year's growth, care is needed in pruning. My own experience is with the yellow form:

R. banksiae lutea which arrived in Britain in 1824 and has similar characteristics to the white, but is butter-yellow in the flowers which have a delicate fragrance. Growing rampantly in all directions and unobstructed in the southerly sun, it has to be kept in check. Most years, it runs neck and neck with Canary Bird (page 26) to begin mass flowering in the first week in May. It has *Wistaria chinensis* (what could be more proper?) as a foil, but somehow the effect does not seem to be successful. Perhaps the foliage ought to be darker, or I should be happier with the white form.

R. bracteata, 1793, the **Macartney Rose**, named after Lord Macartney who headed a trade mission to China in 1792. The secretary of this mission, Sir George Staunton, in a subsidiary activity, collected the climber on a flower-discovery expedition. In 1799, a plant was sent to Thomas Jefferson and as a result of this, subsequent importations and suitability of environment it has become something of an eradication problem in the southern states of America. So says Shepherd, but he points to a positive side, namely, that its underground stems and shoots make it well adapted to prevent soil erosion. The floral beauty of large, single, creamy-white blooms showing golden stamens, and their continuity of production is enhanced by the thick, oval, shining and shrubby foliage. This develops slowly up to 20ft in height, and is therefore best left unpruned. The flowers, singly and in clusters, have fragrance. Shepherd adds that it 'slightly resembles the aroma of an over-ripe apricot': a statement which not many gardeners in the British Isles will be able to check. *R. bracteata*'s chief right to claim our notice is through what amounts to its only offspring (also best left unpruned):

Mermaid, 1918. This resulted when the Macartney Rose was crossed, by William Paul, with an unknown yellow Tea Rose to give, in the right conditions, an outstandingly beautiful climber. Not less than twenty-six nurserymen stock it. The right conditions are not all that onerous – sunny walls, frost-free – therefore less good in the north than in the south, where the foliage may be evergreen. In the adverse conditions of a severe winter, it can be cut down to ground level. It is superior to its parent in freedom of growth, 25ft, in the glossy dark green foliage and in flowers, which are large, single, fragrant and buttercup-yellow. To the latter can be added the facility of retaining the beauty of the stamens after the petals have dropped. Apart from what is said above, all that one can say against Mermaid is that its stems are rather brittle and are heavily, if not viciously, armed.

R. filipes Kiftsgate. This species climber, *R. filipes*, was brought out of western China by E. H. Wilson in 1908. The Kiftsgate records the Gloucestershire garden where it was found in 1954, having been purchased *c* 1938 from the late E. A. Bunyard who, Graham Thomas suggests, secured it from Roseraie de l'Haÿ. The interlacing shoots in youth are tinted brown and copper. In maturity they climb and scramble to a height between 30 and 35ft up trees or over hedges, bearing light green leaves and in July corymbs composed of hundreds of scented, single, creamy-white blossoms. These show orange-yellow stamens and are carried on firm slender stalks – thread-like – hence *filipes*. They make a wonderful sight, as do the myriads of tiny red heps that follow. It takes time, however, to get established: mine, on the completion of its third year, has reached 18ft on its single stem and I have yet to see a flower. Warned, I began with the equally impressive but more speedy and reliable:

R. longicuspis, 1915, also from western China. Flowering towards the end of

July, it is similar to Kiftsgate. The myriads of flowers are a deep cream in the bud and open to milk white. The heps are scarlet or orange-red and the foliage is bold, the leaves being dark glossy green on dark reddish-brown shoots.

R. longicuspis

The flowers are borne in the same way as those of *R. filipes*, but have a fragrance of bananas. After a life of some seven years it is about 20ft and well on its way to taking over the apple tree which supports it and displays astonishing beauty. However, comparing the description of this variety in the *Dictionary of Roses* with that given to *R. filipes* Kiftsgate, I must hope that my life will extend to making my own objective comparison. Incidentally, *R. longicuspis* is said to be often confused with its barely available relative *R. sinowilsonii*, which was introduced by E. H. Wilson (see Kiftsgate) in 1904 and refers to his nickname, 'Chinese Wilson'. Anyway the climber needs the protection of a west wall. Although it did not arrive until 1951, a hybrid of *R. sinowilsonii* must be noticed. It is:

Wedding Day which was raised by Sir Frederick Stern in his 'chalk garden' at Highdown, Sussex (see *highdownensis*, page 46) in 1950. The pointed buds of the single flowers are apricot, opening to a pale creamy-yellow which goes to white. Unfortunately, they tend to spot after rain and become blotched with pink on fading. The growth, which includes a remarkable display of the blooms in clusters and the glossy, rich green foliage, is rampant and can reach 25ft. Clearly it is in the genre of *R. longicuspis* and is said to be a relative of and an improvement on that variety, and of *R. filipes*.

There are others too, and all are suitable for tree climbing and hedge scrambling, or indeed just allowing them to grow into a foaming mound:

R. helenae, found in central China in 1900, this is not quite so exuberant at 18ft, but it has the richly fragrant single cream flowers in abundance and consequently a similar crop of small red heps. The foliage is dark green. One almost says, 'naturally', it was discovered by Chinese Wilson.

Lykkefund, 1930, is a hepless seedling of *R. helenae*, with semi-double flowers in creamy yellow and a salmon tint. It fades to near white. Very fragrant too. The growth, which is thornless, can reach 20ft and the foliage is small, dark and glossy: see in this connection the comment on the Yellow Banksian Rose (page 112). As its name suggests, it was identified in Denmark (1930). Also related to *R. helenae* is:

R. rubus (R. ernestii) which is a tremendous grower to 30ft. The buds often have a rosy tint which, on their opening, becomes a deep cream with orange-yellow suffused at the base of the petals. Add orange stamens and one finds that the dense trusses provide a rich colour effect with an orange fragrance. The correct botanical name for the *R. rubus* described is said to be *R. rubus nudescens*.

Sombreuil, 1851, although a climbing tea rose, is quite hardy and vigorous on a warm wall or fence up to 12ft. The flowers come recurrently, are of great beauty in creamy-white with a flesh-tinted centre, and have a delicious tea fragrance. They have been likened to a refined Souvenir de la Malmaison with its flat and quartered blooms. Mlle Marie de Sombreuil, 1774–c 1823, was a true heroine of the French Revolution. She having, it is said, followed her old father, Governor of 'des Invalides', into the Prison de l'Abbaye and avoided the massacres there by drinking a glass of blood.

MUSK ROSES

Judging by the amount written about *R. moschata* and its hybrids, it should be a terribly important and popular rose, the more so as its age is put as prior to 1600, and the fragrance of 'musk' is said to have completely disappeared from the musk plant of the cottage garden – *mimulas moschatus*. Rivers wrote as late as 1872: 'The White Musk Rose is one of the oldest inhabitants of our gardens, and probably more widely spread over the face of the earth than any other rose.' It is referred to by Shakespeare, Bacon, Milton and Keats, but some have it that actually they wrote about *R. arvensis*. It is highly regrettable that any demand in the UK can be met by only one or at most two nurserymen. The situation seems to be no better in the USA.

R. moschata, the true wild species, the flowers of which do not come until late summer and continue into the autumn. They are white, single and the petals reflex rapidly and are carried on large trusses, but do not produce any heps. The musk fragrance is much in evidence. The leaves are on the small side and oval. The plant can reach 10–12ft and likes plenty of sun. Apparently it has come to light again in the UK only in recent years and been overlaid, overborne and replaced by a hybrid, referred to as a 'botanical garden form' from its magnificent size, up to 50ft, and display, in the gardens at Kew and Cambridge. Only one nursery-man seems to stock it in the UK and that under the name *Rosa moschata floribunda* – one which I have not been able to find in any of the books available to me – but the description fits that of the hybrid in height, form, colour and time of flowering.

I much wish that I could finish this present task of *R. moschata* – one I began solely from a sense of duty to gardeners and others who have such nostalgic feelings for musk roses – but there is more to come:

R. brunonii or **Himalayan Musk Rose** or **R. moschata nepalensis**; but the connection with *R. moschata* is not generally accepted. Powerfully fragrant, single, creamy-white flowers (followed by heps) come in masses in the summer months. The foliage is a dull grey-green. Growth is very vigorous, about 40ft, but not hardy and thus needs a sunny, sheltered situation. Apropos of the foregoing about the *moschata* hybrid's having been taken to be the true *R. moschata*, the only pro-vider of *R. brunonii* says: 'Often wrongly grown in cultivation as *R. moschata*.'

La Mortola, 1954, described as a particularly fine form of *R. brunonii*, this, if one so requires, will fill a space measuring 3ft × 40ft, over wall, hedge or tree. It makes the common demand for full sun and a mild climate. The flowers are creamy-white. As singles they show their yellow stamens and are full of musk fragrance.

Paul's Himalayan Musk Rambler seems to be another in the ilk of vigorous summer florescence and growth, 30ft. The flowers are, however, blush lilac-pink and double. Like *R. filipes* and *R. longicuspis* it is splendid for growing in trees. Anyway, two nurserymen in England think it worth offering, as they do La Mortola.

The Garland, 1835, is recorded as a hybrid from *R. moschata* × *multiflora* and, as might be expected, it has a very pleasant fragrance from the multitude of semi-double creamy-salmon buds which open to cream faintly 'blushed' and fading to creamy-white. The petals are 'quilled' and there are some yellow stamens. The fragrance is that of an orange; and there are small oval red heps. An important thing to note is that no matter at what angle the trusses of flowers grow, the flower stalks grow erect, so that all the flowers are upright. I have had one in my garden, well over 15ft, for years until in 1973 Graham Thomas came and said it was not The Garland but the Rambling Rector, about which one can read on page 118.

It may be odd to deal with the matter in a chapter on climbers, but before leaving the Musk Roses a word must be said about the comparatively well-known group of shrubs, the so-called **Hybrid Musks.** 'So-called' seems justified, because the *R. moschata* element in their pedigree is obscure and slight. In particular, in the context of this book, they are neither wild nor old garden roses. The (fore)father of them all did not arrive until 1904 and the first comer to the group was *c* 1913 and the last 1950. They are splendid shrubs but out of place here. In so deciding I am prevented from dealing with **Francis E. Lester,** an American (1946) climbing seedling from a hybrid musk and one of my garden joys. (See page 103 where it is climbing, hand over hand, up a Lawson's Cypress.)

MULTIFLORAS

R. multiflora. Although the source of supply in Britain seems to be limited to one nurseryman only, this may be growing in many gardens because it is used as an understock, as is *R. canina,* on which nurserymen bud the hybrid teas, floribundas and the like. If, unfortunately, the rose weakens or dies back, then the understock usually takes over and one has *R. multiflora japonica.* It can be recognised from the quite small, single, creamy flowers – fading to white – with bright yellow stamens producing a 'fruity' fragrance. The fruit is unidentified, but the fragrance is really quite pleasant. The flowers come in 'rambler-like' trusses, followed by tiny red heps: the growing habit is similar, as it can make a mound of arching stems to 12ft or climb a tree up to 20ft. It has been much used by American nurserymen since 1902 as an understock; indeed, it seems as popular there as *R. canina* is in the British Isles for that purpose. It is also being used for informal hedges, again particularly in the USA, where it has been advertised as 'horsehigh, bull strong, and goat tight' and more economical than wire, as well as a windbreak to reduce erosion of the soil. Another use in the USA and which has been urged in Britain, is, unsurprisingly, for barriers on motorways.

There are various forms which need not concern us, but *multiflora japonica* is basically the same as the one known as **Polyantha Simplex,** first used as an understock in Europe *c* 1880. There are, however, some hybrids of garden value most of which are of early twentieth-century origin, but I operate my self-imposed rule, flexibility, on account of their 'old garden rose' colours. The first, however, is within it.

Polyantha Grandiflora, 1886, has botanical complications about its name, but it seems probable that it is R. *multiflora* crossed with a garden variety. Summer-flowering, its blooms are single, creamy-white with orange stamens borne in clusters on which follow oval, medium-sized, orange-red heps. Their orange fragrance is strong. The foliage is smooth-leafed, tinted in youth, deep green and deep-veined in maturity. The stems have sparse reddish thorns and can ramble or climb up to 15ft.

Rambling Rector has no date of origin, but the name is charming. He is adjudged to be almost pure R. *multiflora*, but for the flowers which are semi-double. They come in great quantity and are cream to begin with, but fade to white, as the yellow stamens turn dark. The strong fragrance is like that of R. *multiflora*. By the time this is read I hope that I shall have really made up my mind (see page 103) whether it is the coarser Rambling Rector or The Garland in my garden.

Goldfinch, 1907, is also claimed to be almost pure *multiflora* from the garden point of view because that wild rose is on both sides of its parentage; Helenae (page 115) is mixed up in it. It ought to be encouraged because of the strong fragrance: not only of oranges but of bananas too. The bearers of this exotic combination begin with yolk-yellow and, in hot sunshine, end milk-white with dark yellow stamens. If they are cut in the bud for the house, the fading to milk-white can be avoided. The light green foliage goes very well with the clusters of yolk-yellow blooms on stems which can reach 12ft.

Veilchenblau, 1909. I remember my first sight of this *multiflora* rambler so well. It was at a time when I was immersed in the modern roses and those of the old garden types were almost unknown. I thought it very odd and distinctly 'old hat'. I certainly did not imagine that within less than ten years I should be wondering what all the fuss and speculation (in the gardening media) over a 'blue' rose was all about, knowing that a 'blue' rambler already existed. And, more importantly, I liked it very much. Perhaps it did in fact trigger off, with delayed action, my love for the violets, maroons, magentas, purples, lilacs and lavender blues of the nineteenth century. Anyway, I like to think so, because the violet, dark magenta, maroon, lilac-grey petals, with a streak of white of Veilchenblau, can be seen 20ft and more up among the trees in my own garden. Here they happily inter-mingle their green-apple fragrance with the light scent from the pure white, semi-double flowers of a much overlooked 1917 climber – **Purity**. The debt to Veilchenblau is increased by its seedling:

Violette, 1921, whose clustering flowers are crimson-purple, maroon-purple, maroon-grey, set off by yellow stamens. On the other side of the garden to that of her forebear, she goes very well with Souvenir de la Malmaison and William Lobb, but the experts say I should do better with large single pinks, such as Lady Curzon (page 56) or Complicata (page 67). To intrude a 1924 rambler is perhaps pushing flexibility a bit far, but this beautiful one must be recorded:

Rose-Marie Viaud or, if one wishes, **Améthyste.** Light green foliage sets off amethyst-magenta-pink flowers, especially in the sunlight or, if one so prefers, the colours are vivid cerise on opening, going on to pure parma-violet and ending even paler. It has stout thornless stems which can reach 15ft and then arch over, or, in a tree, hang down in festoons bearing large bunches of scentless, fully double, rosette-like flowers. It does, most usefully, flower later than the other violet ramblers.

Even writing a book enlarges one's own experience. Good fortune has given the space and the trees, but the future does not provide sufficient time: were this otherwise I would have Veilchenblau, Violette and Rose-Marie Viand together or adjacent to each other with Purity or a white or creamy multiflora, such as the Rambling Rector or Polyantha Grandiflora, in between.

NOISETTIANAS OR NOISETTE ROSES

Here we have, for a change, a simple and straightforward story of origin which comes from Shepherd, who says that the original Noisette was the result of a cross between *R. chinensis* and *R. moschata* and that it was the first major contribution by an American hybridist to the rose family. It fell to one John Champneys, a lover of roses, by profession a rice grower, of Charleston, South Carolina to produce prior to 1817, from the cross mentioned, a pink cluster climber. He gave cuttings of the seedling to Philip C. Noisette, a local florist who, perceiving the floral value and commercial possibilities, began intensive propagation and breeding. In 1817 he sent seeds from the original cuttings to his brother Louis in Paris: he named the most promising seedling from these seeds, **Le Rosier de Philip Noisette.** There were of course other plants from this sowing, which being hybrids showed differences to a greater or lesser degree, and several were named. Included with the seeds Philip sent to Louis was a seedling he himself had raised from a, naturally, pollinated seed from his **Pink Cluster**: this he had labelled 'Blush'. The flowers were more double than those of the original, and the growth was more dwarf and compact. It was named **Blush Noisette** and is still available today. It is offered as a semi-climber or loosely growing shrub with good foliage to 10ft, and gives flowers recurrently in clusters, with a clove fragrance.

The French took up the production of the noisettes with enthusiasm and introduced tea roses into their crosses. The 1864–5 catalogue of Paul & Son lists thirty varieties. These have left us, as we shall see, three famous climbers, pretty far removed from the original noisettes, but usually treated as members of that group. All except two were in Paul's catalogues covering 1864–96: the largest number of noisettes shown during that period did not exceed thirty.

Desprez à fleur jaune, 1835, is a really good garden climber, recurrent-flowering to an extent that can almost justify the adjective 'perpetual'. It comes from a cross between the Blush Noisette and Park's Yellow Tea-scented China (no longer obtainable) and gives a warm yellow bloom shaded or flushed with peach and apricot. The fragrance is fruity too. The flowers are flat and the plentiful petals centred with a button eye. It needs the sun and is therefore at its best on a warm wall, where its zig-zag growth can reach 15ft, arch over and produce the flowers on every shoot, one of which is produced at each turn of the stems.

Céline Forestier, 1842, is a second generation from a tea cross. The flowers are in the superlative class. They open flat and wide to show quartered petals, a button eye, and pale yellow with tones of peach in colour. In all, it is of high quality, but at the price of slow growth and, not unsurprisingly, good soil and a warm wall, when it may reach 12ft.

There will be criticism if I do not mention the famous 'tea-noisette':

Maréchal Niel, 1864, but really this is for a greenhouse, where the tea-scented, buttery-yellow loose double blooms and their fragrance will be at their best. Its vigorous growth of up to 15ft will need a large greenhouse, or a good deal of manipulation in a small one. The blooms come on weak stalks and nod accordingly. It is said to flower outdoors in a sheltered position on a warm wall in warm districts. As these sites are fully occupied in my garden and the very small greenhouse is in the same condition with a grape-vine, I fear that the Maréchal's pleasures must be foregone, despite the fact that it is still in demand. Even more in demand, and understandably, is:

Gloire de Dijon, 1853, which requires no shelter and so on, but gives, with great and constant recurrency, its buff-yellow flowers, which in warm weather can also show pink and apricot and give off a rich fragrance. It certainly requires support, as the growth to 15–18ft is slender and leggy, but from experience I do not recommend using an apple tree: it disappears into the thick foliage, which allows only an occasional glimpse of the blooms. Clearly a wall is infinitely better, especially if the bareness of the base is covered by other plants – roses or other shrubs. There is no difficulty in buying it in Britain: one has the choice of nearly twenty nurserymen.

Fellemberg, 1857, is classed as a noisette because its character is pretty close to the Blush Noisette plus that of the larger growing Chinas. Like Céline Forestier, it takes time to build up to full growth of 8ft. The flowers are smallish, semi-double, cupped and crimson-pink: they come very freely and recurrently in clusters of various sizes, smelling like sweet peas. The young leaves are a purplish green and mature to dark green. It goes well with other shrubs, but is not for the front of the border or bed. An even greater quantity of bloom is forthcoming if it is kept pruned down to 3ft.

Mme Alfred Carrière, 1879, has parentage attributions as varied as the meanings of her name and her qualities are in like measure. Light green foliage sets off rounded, cupped flowers of blush creamy-white having a delicious fragrance. Grown on a wall it can reach 25ft, or left to its own devices as a bush it can be 12ft × 12ft. It is 'seldom without a few blooms in October'. I was writing this one November day when my wife brought in a whitish bloom, saying: 'I have discovered a label on this rose which I asked you about some time ago. It is Mme Alfred Carrière.' I agreed and apologised for not remembering that it had been put in during the previous April. Does it really matter from what or where an old rose variety came, if it is a really good rose, which answers to what is claimed for it? Paul & Son did not seem to think so: they invariably included it in a short list headed: 'Climbing Varieties Not Necessarily Show Sorts'. Mark you, had they put it among the 'Noisette Roses' it would have followed an entry labelled 'La Biche'. They did, however, include it in that list and again in the same catalogue, 1898, under 'Miscellaneous Climbing Roses – Some Novelties of Merit':

Alister Stella Gray, 'a continuous bloomer, flowering from June to November; yellow, of great excellence and beauty, a glorious Pillar Rose.' Eighty years later this claim continues to be admitted. The buds are yolk-yellow in the centre, fading later to cream. They come in early summer, two or three together at the end of each shoot, in perfection of shape and of tea-rose fragrance which continues in the quartered blooms with a button centre. The vigorous growth is similar to that of Desprez à fleur Jaune, with the flowers at the ends of the zig-zagging stems. Yet with it all, only two nurseries in England offer this lovely climber, which against a wall can reach to 15ft or better, or as a loose bush 8ft. In the USA the name is **Golden Rambler,** and one hopes that it is better appreciated there.

SEMPERVIRENS

R. *sempervirens* is a wild species found in North Africa and southern Europe. As the name indicates, it is evergreen or practically so. It may be growing in gardens in the British Isles, but is not on offer by any nursery. It was used for hybridisation mainly in France, and there by M Jacques – the gardener to the Duc d'Orléans – who raised in 1827 the only hybrid now generally known and freely available in the UK:

Félicité et Perpétue is not only freely available to buy, but is freely used in country villages in England and Wales. A true rambler with charming creamy-white pompon-shaped flowers, carried singly and in clusters. The 'once-only' crop is best seen trained up to 12ft and left to sprawl over. I had three fine specimens grown from cuttings kindly given me when on a visit to Roath Park, Cardiff. They grew as mounding bushes 7–8ft high. For many years I much admired and was rather proud of my Félicité et Perpétues. Then the expert came, and that ended that variety; but, naturally, being an expert he could not say what it was, except probably one of the multifloras. My usual good fortune held: late in the following spring came a gift of half a dozen rose plants, one labelled Félicité et Perpétue. It has yet to flower but judged by the foliage, which is small, dark green and glossy, the expert is right. All that remains is to search the books for that unknown multiflora, whose foliage certainly does not answer that description.

By the way, St Felicitas and St Perpetua were Carthaginian martyrs and gave their names to the rose, so it is said, via two daughters of the Duc d'Orléans. The saint's day is 7 May, but – as will be understood – I cannot as yet say whether it has any significance in relation to the rose's date of flowering.

WICHURAIANAS

R. wichuraiana, in itself makes a first-rate garden rose and its qualities are carried in most respects into its progeny. It ought to be more widely grown in Britain: in the USA it is known as the **Memorial Rose**, owing to its use in cemeteries. It can be trained upright on supports, such as trees or bushes, up to 15ft or more. Thereafter the trailing shoots can be allowed to cascade down to show in August clusters of small, single, white flowers with yellow stamens and a sweet fragrance. It is, however, *par excellence* (as are most of its offspring) a wonderful ground coverer, as it grows prostrate, with self-rooting trailing stems which also bear small, glossy, dark green leaves; it is evergreen in habit.

R. wichuraiana was, as Shepherd writes, discovered in Japan by a German botanist, Dr Max Ernst Wichura, in 1861. It was an important discovery in influencing future roses, but he may not have realised it as such when sending plants to Germany. These apparently did not survive; but successors did so in Munich and Brussels in 1880 and were named after the discoverer, then dead, in 1886 by Crépin, a Belgian botanist. Plants reached the Arnold Arboretum in Massachusetts, USA, in 1888 and from there rooted layers came to Kew Gardens, England, in 1890. Other sources suggest that it arrived direct from Japan a year later. Be this as it may, it was the Americans who first got cracking in the production of hybrids, with their hardy vigorous growth and clustering flowers. Michael H. Horvath is the name most associated with these early days, and the results of his work were put out in 1898 and 1899 by his former employers – Pitcher & Manda Nursery of New Jersey. In 1901 Jackson & Perkins of Newark, NY introduced Dorothy Perkins, which brings us to the twentieth century in which the French, as in Barbier et Compagnie of Orleans, were forming their own group, which includes a number of well-known varieties to be added to those of the US hybridists.

The latter include in addition to Dorothy Perkins: May Queen (a 1898 relic), Excelsa, American Pillar, Breeze Hill, Dr van Fleet and its recurrent-flowering New Dawn; Mary Wallace, and Silver Moon.

To the French we owe: Albéric Barbier, Albertine, François Juranville, Léontine Gervais, Paul Transon.

We began (page 62) with Alain Blanchard, as an illustration of the intermingling and continuity of the various sorts of roses. I think it would be pleasant to end with another. It is:

R. *dupontii*, which as 'Dupont' may by now be a name not unfamiliar to readers. To what has been said earlier one would now add that he is credited with being the first recorded person to produce an artificial hybrid rose, ie, man-manipulated. He may have produced the variety of his name, which, but for the foregoing, would have followed on R. *moschata*, page 116, because it comes from a cross with that variety and R. *gallica*. It gives the best of both parents: for me, a lover of single and near single, roses, it ranks very highly with clear white petals, following a pink tint, well rounded, that is, convex, giving them a distinct 'sculptured', ie three-dimensioned, shape – one which I regard as much superior to that o Nevada's blooms (page 46).

The greyish-green matt foliage fits well and for fragrance it offers bananas and for size 7ft × 7ft.

A beautiful rose to end on, but life is not like that. The better one knows a rose the more likely one is to forget it. Pray forgive me, but under the 'Alba Roses' should have appeared: **Belle Amour,** with its cupped semi-double coral pink blooms accompanied by fragrance of spice and giving interesting heps. It carries dark grey-green foliage up to 6ft × 4ft. Said to have been found in a convent garden at Elboeuf, a place I know well, situated not as some learned rose writers would seem to have it, in Germany, but on a bend in the Seine between Rouen and Le Havre.

CHAPTER II

HOW THEY CAN BE USED

I am afraid that my own collection of wild and old garden roses has, as already indicated, been gathered together in an haphazard way: it is still in the process of being sorted out, but is currently nearing completion.

As regards the wild species roses, it has already been mentioned how well they fit in with other garden shrubs. Indeed, it has been shown (page 41) how, quite happily – even if fortuitously – this can come about. I mention here how the rugosas listed on pages 50–5 make excellent combinations with hydrangeas of all kinds.

I find or, with modesty, I think that my own garden provides a useful and practical illustration not only of how the wild roses can be used in conjunction with other plants, but also of how those plants can be used with the old garden roses.

THE WILD GARDEN

By undeservedly good fortune I have a wild garden of some 60yd × 11yd. It is limited by a mixed hedge and a line of cypress, birch, ash and hawthorn trees. In it is growing the major portion of my wild roses, with a sprinkling of moss roses, and that rightly banished Conrad F. Meyer (page 55) which, I am glad to say, seems to have realised by this penitential treatment its iniquities and greatly curtailed the propensity to produce diseases. Added to and mixed with the roses are, fortuitously, quite a few of the shrubs and plants which fit happily, at any rate with me, into a wild garden.

They are – my wife being that departmental expert and in her walking order –

Iris foetidissima, grown for its brilliant orange-red seeds; ajuga (or common bugle); polyanthus; *anemone blanda*; *kolkwitzia pulmonaria*; *primula*; violets (blue and white); *bergenia delavayi*; *berberis darwinii*; *campanula garganica*; valerian (if you have it, you always have it); foxgloves; hostas, and in particular – grandiflora, *sieboldiana*, *undulata* and *fortunei*; *helleborus corsicus*; *helleborus niger*; *weigela*; *hypericum* Rowallane; *montbretia*; *antholyza paniculatus*; *lamium*; *senecio laxifolius* and White Diamond.

To this list is added such partial-shade accepting plants as *aquilegia*, *asperula*, *digitalis*, honesty, *meconopsis*, *myosotis*, hardy species primulas, primroses and *verbascum*.

The naturals for the front and more sunny positions are of course arabis, aubrieta, alyssum saxatile, pansies, pinks, violas, nepeta, cheiranthus and wall-flowers.

Consult a comprehensive seed list and one will be most pleasantly surprised at the number of the foregoing plants which can be raised from seed sown in open ground and, therefore, at a very moderate cost per plant.

Narcissus, the botanical name for daffodils, which are with the many other bulbs my own particular interest: I cannot emphasise too much how important they are in relation to roses of all kinds, especially when the roses are planted in formal beds.

Bulbs are not expensive when one realises that they can repeat themselves year after year and, if they are the naturalising kind, can increase enormously in number. Moreover, 'bulbs' are not just 'daffodils', 'crocuses', 'tulips' and 'hyacinths'. The latter are much associated with bowls in the house and tulips, as far as I am concerned, are much too 'grenadier-like' for a country garden. Kaufmannianas are, however, acceptable; as would be the species tulips if one could afford them.

If I may say so, much is missed if the lesser known bulbs are neglected, particularly when (as the following list shows) they can give flowers from winter to early summer:

January: Snowdrops (*Galanthus*); Winter Aconites (*Eranthis*)

February: Species crocus. I use especially Blue Pearl, Cream Beauty, E. A. Bowles, Zwanenburg Bronze, *Susianus*, *Tomasinianus*, *Iris reticulata* and *Danfordiae*

March: *Anemone blanda* (not very successful with me); *Chionodoxa* (very good when planted in clumps or among daffodils); Dutch crocus

April: *Cyclamen repandum*, daffodils and narcissi; Dog's Tooth Violet (*erythronium*); Grape Hyacinths (*muscari*) and Snake's-head Lily (*fritillaria meleagris*)

May: *Camassia esculenta* (Bear Grass); Dutch Iris, *Ornithogalum umbellatum* (Star of Bethlehem), wonderful naturalisers; Pheasant Eye narcissus; Scillas (Bluebells) in variety

June: *Allium Moly*; *Brodiaea*; English and Spanish Iris

All the foregoing bulbs have their place in the wild garden with the wild and old garden roses. My wife and I are not fanatical or precision gardeners, neither can finance be disregarded. What we have learnt is by a little reading, by much experience accumulated over the years and based on the original design devised by Dame Sylvia Crowe. We would have arrived at our present pleasure from the wild garden, to a much greater degree and much earlier if Judith Berrisford's *The Wild Garden* (1966) had come our way not months but years ago. As it is one can only recommend it wholeheartedly to gardeners who are interested in getting the maximum pleasure from gardens of that kind.

And that maximum pleasure includes the roses, old and new – hybrid teas and floribundas – which can well profit from the interplanting and, therefore, from restriction of weeds, especially from plants which give of their blooms before the roses produce their own. Such plants can be selected from those mentioned above and, more particularly and exhaustively, from Judith Berrisford's book. Remember, for example, that when planting is carried out among roses, old and new, the dying-off and yellowing foliage of the daffodils and narcissi will be obscured by the foliage of the roses.

I end with some advice: it is that having decided how much one can afford to spend each year on bulbs (and to a lesser extent on plants), do not spread it over in small quantities of many kinds and varieties. If, say, you have £5 or £10 available annually, put the whole of it into one variety of daffodils or crocuses, ornithogalums or whatever interests you. In that way you will build up a worthwhile show. If you put this tip to Roy Hay you would find that he agreed with it. Remember too that 'mixtures' are usually cheaper and also, in my experience, the mixture is not mixed, but the constituent varieties tend to come in 'layers'. So if these are planted as they come, one is likely to get clumps, very nearly, of the same kinds.

The other advice is very short: weedkillers are *not* for the wild garden. This I learnt from bitter experience, having read Judith Berrisford's warning too late.

THE OLD GARDEN ROSES

Clearly a great deal of the foregoing applies to the use of the old garden varieties: indeed it was introduced by the quotation from Rivers on page 76. And from Nancy Steen's *Charm of Old Roses* we are ourselves in the process of raising fuchsias, from cuttings, to interplant with the old garden roses.

I will say that the latter mix in well with most other shrubs and plants; and a large bed or border so mixed can be a great pleasure. But for the purist one can do very well with confining oneself to the old garden roses by a judicious mixing (and they do mix) of the recurrent-flowering varieties, mainly the bourbons and hybrid perpetuals, with the varieties which offer their florescence in one period only. Alternatively, for the latter, there is a way of prolonging the flowering period somewhat: it is to prune (Chapter 12) an established plant as to one half in November and the other half in March or early April.

'Pegging-down' has been mentioned earlier in the descriptions of some varieties; it can help towards greater florescence. Other suitable varieties are also included in Appendix A.

Those with lax growth can support each other by close planting, but can be effectively trained on fences, walls and pillars. Some including, more particularly, wild roses and climbers can be used for sprawling ground cover and for covering tree stumps and such like.

THE CLIMBERS

One hopes that enough has been said in that section to indicate the potentiality of the 'old' climbers, compared with the modern sorts. Most can be 'scramblers', as well as climbers, over hedges, tree stumps and over the ground. Most are once-flowering, but what a flowering.

Here I can introduce one of the two basic principles on which my garden is run. It is that in general the wild, old garden and climbing roses are allowed to get on with it under their own steam: this means no tying up. The modern climbers may be twisted round horizontal wires. The old ones may get one starting twist of twine round a tree trunk, but thereafter they are at large. And, despite quoted widths, old garden bush types are planted close enough to enable the old ladies and gentlemen to hold each other up – or mostly so.

We can now move on in comfortable sequence to the use of all three kinds – wild, old garden and climbers – for hedges and in the house.

Hedges. The varieties of R. *rugosa* (pages 53–4) are 'naturals', with their solidity from their abundant growth and foliage as found in the alba, Frau Dagmar Hastrup, Roseraie de l'Haÿ and Scabrosa. The hybrids Sarah van Fleet and Lady Curzon can be useful too. All of them are recurrent-flowering, and as already noted, give added beauty in the autumn from colour changes in the foliage and some from their heps, page 34.

Very different in shape and of smaller size, but in my view very desirable, are R. *virginiana* and its counterpart R. *v. alba*. So too, mostly, in like size is R. *spinosissima* and its larger relatives, such as S. *altaica*, S. *bicolor*, the double white and Frühlingsgold, which being somewhat more open is particularly useful as a taller screen. So also are R. *cantabrigiensis* and R. *highdownensis* – each planted at about 4ft intervals.

From what has been said in their individual descriptions, one would be right in thinking that, especially when used on wires, and widely spaced, R. *macrantha*, R. *paulii* and, to a lesser extent, R. *paulii rosea*, also R. *gallica* Complicata, could be very effective.

At 3ft apart sturdy, self-supporting hedges can be obtained from Dupontii, the albas such as *alba maxima*, Belle Amour, Great Maiden's Blush; the moss rose, Capitaine John Ingram and the bourbon, Louise Odier.

But excellent and floriferous hedges can be got from such varieties as the gallicas – Belle de Crécy, Charles de Mills, *officinalis*, Tuscany Superb, Rosa Mundi – planted 2ft apart and clipped back with shears in late winter.

For boundary and field hedges one cannot do better than use R. *rubiginosa* at 3ft apart or R. *multiflora* somewhat closer.

These suggestions have been brought together in Appendix A.

In the house. It has been recorded elsewhere that modern roses are not terribly long-lasting in the house. But expert opinion – Elizabeth Churchill – has it, and I agree, that the length of life of most rose blooms in the house approximates to that of their life on the bush.

On the other hand, the same authority – an expert in flower arrangement too – did not accept a statement that many people who find satisfaction from that activity, grew the wild and old garden roses solely in pursuit of their art. She has it, and again I would agree, that the real incentive is in the luscious colours and fragrance of the flowers – in the garden or anywhere else.

One finds with pleasure her specially recommending, when they are cut in the 'colour-showing' bud stage: Boule de Neige (page 93); Fantin-Latour (page 77); Du Maître d'École (page 67); Charles de Mills (page 65); and Königen von Dänemark (page 70).

There does not seem to be any book specially directed to the use of the wild and old garden roses in flower arrangements, but those which can be quite useful are *My Roses* by Julia Clements, and *A Modern Herbal* and *Flower Arrangements From Wild Plants* both written by Violet Stevenson.

CHAPTER 12

SOIL PREPARATION, PLANTING, PRUNING AND CULTURAL CARE

All that the reader knows from experience, my own and other books, about the soil and its preparation in relation to modern roses applies to the wild and old garden roses too. To sum up: they like slightly acid soil – pH 5·6–6·5, but will do equally well, in my experience, in the lower alkaline readings in the pH scale, say 7 and somewhat above.

If one begins from scratch then the best preparation is, as for modern varieties, to double-dig – more correctly called bastard trenching – the soil. The object being to break up both the top soil and the second spit, but taking care to leave the top soil at the top because this is the most fertile. Full details of bastard trenching will be found in most garden books – it is much easier to do than to read about. If one has old manure or compost it is no bad thing to stir some into that *second* spit. Also if time and weather conditions allow, let the bed, that is the soil, settle down before beginning to plant the roses. This really means that September–October is the best time to make new beds or prepare existing ones for roses. It is not a good thing to put new rose plants into beds which have long contained roses. Nor, indeed, if one wishes to put wild or old garden roses among other shrubs or plants can one recommend that it is sufficient just to dig a hole sufficiently large to take the plant and then put it in.

Treatment on arrival – 'Heeling in'. Clearly the sooner the package is open and the new arrivals are in the ground, the better. Frost, snow, sodden ground or lack of time may clearly say wait: so, leave the package unopened. Sheltered from frost the plants will be quite safe for up to a fortnight. If, however, adverse conditions are likely to be prolonged, then open up and 'heel' the plants in by making a shallow trench, laying the roots therein and covering them and the lower part of the stems with soil, which should be lightly firmed down.

Heeled in, the plants will remain in excellent condition for a long time, especially if one has removed any foliage still on them. Should, however, something go wrong, do not despair if your plants have dried out and shrivelled up. Bury them *completely* about a spit deep and they will be completely restored in about 10–14 days.

If the planting operation is to be 'straight from package to bed', it will be very beneficial to immerse the roots in water for an hour or so. It follows that during the actual planting work the roots of the plants waiting attention should be kept covered with a sack or something to prevent them drying out. This is most important and, of course, applies also to plants which have been heeled in.

Importance of planting operation. Proper planting is a much more important element in successful rose growing than many other things which we are enjoined to do. Moreover, it is surely worth while taking trouble over plants which, normally, will be good for at least 12–20 years.

The use of a planting mixture is an essential ingredient in the operation. Personally I use one consisting of a double handful of sterilised bone-meal added to a three-gallon bucket of moist peat and mixed in. If, however, I was more up to date and affluent a handful of hoof and horn would be added. The mixing is best done in the wheelbarrow or some other large receptacle.

The planting operation. Provided with plants, sack, spade and planting mixture, we are ready to begin: but first it may be useful to peg out the positions in the bed that the bushes are going to occupy.

We then make our hole: one of rather over a foot in diameter seems about right, with sufficient depth to ensure that the union – the fattish knobbly junction between the root stock and the rose proper will be not less than three inches *below* the level of the soil when the job is complete. The italics are important, because with ordinary roses one gets the union at ground level. If the plant is on its own roots – certainly many wild roses are – it is usually quite easy to see from the main stem the level at which they were grown in the nursery, take your three inches below that line. (In connection with this deep planting see what has been said on page 54 about how La Belle Portvine has provided an abundance of new rooted growth, despite the fact that it is on a root stock.)

Next insert the bush and spread out the roots evenly if you can, but do not worry if, because they are all pointing one way this cannot be done completely. Just do what can be done – it is quite unnecessary to shout for help because you want two hands to keep the roots spread out – the quality of the plant and its blooms are unlikely to suffer because the roots cannot be fanned out with the precision of the frame of an umbrella.

Having got the plant in the hole add the mixture and soil in alternate handfuls, giving the plant an occasional shake to let them get among the roots. When the hole is becoming full start to firm lightly with hands or foot, adding mixture and soil as necessary, and finish by treading firmly, working from the outside of the hole towards the centre – the reverse process will lower the plant. (This is sometimes a useful get-out if the hole has not been made quite deep enough.)

This description assumes that the soil is in just the right condition: it may not be so. Planting in very heavy soil will be more satisfactory if more peat is used in addition to that of the mixture. If the soil is very wet and sticky and planting cannot wait, then the 'tread in' should be done very lightly indeed and one should wait until the drying winds have put things right before finally firming in. In connection with both these points, some people take steps to keep a supply of dry soil under shelter, which they add to the mixture – half and half.

Really the job of planting is quite straightforward – but I repeat it is certainly worth a little special trouble.

Pruning. Normally it is better to leave the plant untouched at the planting stage, except, possibly, just to trim back to a bud at the end of each shoot. In short: wait and see how it develops.

From what has just been written it will cause no surprise, when I say that, in general, we prune all our roses too much – see in this connection what Sam McGredy has said in Chapter 13 – and that, in particular, whatever we may do about our modern roses, the old 'uns will do best if one treats them lightly.

The young wild ones will need to be watched for shape by encouraging new shoots and, to get flowers and heps, by cutting out old, small twiggy growth. In later years, new growth can be encouraged by cutting out old spent wood. In short, unlike the 'moderns', they need very little pruning.

And that goes for the old garden roses too. Very old wood being cut out to encourage new basal growth, and, at discretion, other growth being shortened by a third of their length. This should give one a smother of flowers on a freely growing bush. If, however, one seeks for perfection of flowers then the side shoots from the main stems should be 'spurred' pruned, that is, cut back to two or three buds.

On the whole, as regards both sorts – wild and old garden – I would say just let them get on with it, but do a good cleaning-up and cut every three or four years.

It is only right to give the other side – especially as it comes from Rivers, whose book I much respect. His pruning would be for –

Gallicas, Albas and Damasks – 'cut out all spray-like shoots, and then shorten, to within six or eight buds of their base all strong shoots ... those above 15in in length; the weak shoots cut down to two or three buds'.

Centifolias and Moss roses – 'every shoot shortened to three or four buds, otherwise the plants soon become straggling and unsightly'.

Bourbons – remove 'all the small branches and their spurs which have produced bloom, and then shortening the shoots to within five or six buds of the base of each'.

Cultural care. This heading is an omnibus one. Taking the pleasant side first – feeding, we have already in the planting mixture touched on two dietetical ingredients: bone-meal producing phosphate, and hoof and horn giving nitrogen; the third essential requirement is potash. Of course, other things are necessary too. For my part I have been through the whole gamut of the mixed fertilisers for roses and have come the full circle: I began with a proprietary fish manure and I am ending with it. Basically it is like, for instance, bone-meal organic, that is, slow-acting, but it is fortified with the quicker-working inorganics. A combination which is, I gather, being increasingly adopted in the many proprietary mixtures specially made up for roses. Of these I prefer, for handling convenience, those in pellet or granular form. In use, just carry out the makers' directions.

Pests and diseases. Here may I, in relation to the roses in this book, echo the not infrequent exhortation of that now well-known British non-commissioned officer who fought at the battle of Omdurman (1898)? 'Don't panic!' If, however, you must, leave it for the next chapter.

No doubt I am fortunate, but the rose pests hardly worry me at all. Aphids are usually the most troublesome to most gardeners, but there is a highly effective and economical natural remedy – squash them with finger and thumb. If 'handwork' is too hard or repulsive then the pesticide malathion gives the best control.

For the rest, such as caterpillars, swinging on their threads, let them have their cut, live and let live. I am, however, bound to say that neither of them seem to be interested in the wild and old varieties. Moreover, they do not seem to worry the moderns either: I, no doubt mistakenly, put this happy condition of affairs to the keen cultivation in the garden of the birds – especially the tits through nesting boxes, peanut kernels and wild bird seeds.

At the beginning of Chapter 4 are outlined briefly the three main diseases of roses. How they inflict themselves on the modern roses is illustrated in Chapter 13. On page 109 is shown how they affect the wild and old garden roses. The former hardly at all: the latter can suffer from mildew and to a much lesser extent from black spot and rust. A warning is noted against the descriptions of the varieties which may be concerned. But seriously, I would not worry until disease strikes. This is said, by one who in his experience of the modern roses can guarantee only two varieties which will be disease free – the hybrid tea: Pink Favourite and the floribunda: Chanelle. And who has seen no disease on his old garden roses, except mildew on two moss roses and black spot on Variegata de Bologna.

For general protection against disease the Royal National Rose Society sprays with Bordeaux mixture in December as a preventive against the carrying over of disease from one year to the next, and then continues to spray with maneb against black spot and rust. The first immediately after pruning followed by regular spraying at 10–14 day intervals, at the first signs of these diseases: when mildew appears dinocap is added. **Always carry out the maker's directions on these and similar products.** Against black spot and rust I spray with maneb and for mildew I find benomyl (benlate) very effective – it seems somewhat less so against black spot unless used as soon as young foliage appears, which is what the distributors recommend. A comparatively new product in the USA for use against mildew, which is said to give good results, is 'Pipion'.

CHAPTER 13

THE ROSES OF TODAY AND THE FUTURE

(including some thoughts of Sam McGredy and Jack Harkness)

We have looked at the varieties of wild and old garden roses currently available to us ordinary gardeners. It has been suggested that – quite apart from their historical significance and their part in the evolution of our present-day roses – on their own garden and floral merits we are losing much beauty and much enjoyment from not using them more freely. This is so despite their size (which covers a much wider range than people think), the low key of some of their unique colours, and production in some but by no means all of only one crop of flowers. On the other hand there is compensation by way of less uniform flower formations, in the wild roses of more decorative foliage, in shape and tone, in fruit in the form of heps, and of fragrance – mainly fruity. Advisedly, fragrance has been put last. If I may say so, too much is said about how the modern hybridist has 'bred out' the fragrance of the old roses, the implication being that modern roses have no fragrance at all or, at best, if there be fragrance it is only a pale reflection of past glory. It is not as bad as all that: in the current list (1974) published by the Royal National Rose Society, of the adjudged twenty-four best hybrid teas over five years old, ten are noted as 'most fragrant'. While for those fifteen varieties which have been available for a lesser period, five receive this comment. If one may put it rather bluntly: the hybridist has no guarantee that any particular cross, even one from two very fragrant parents, will produce fragrant offspring or, indeed, those having any fragrance at all. This aspect is intended here to get it out of the way or, more hopefully, perhaps to reduce this particular criticism to size. In the author's judgement there are far more interesting comparisons to be made between old and modern roses – if indeed comparisons need be made at all.

In the preceding pages we have looked at 81 varieties of wild roses and 124 old garden varieties. They have been selected on the basis that, broadly, they are available from at least two nurserymen in the British Isles and by and large are also available – remembering the very wide range of climatic conditions – in the USA where, incidentally, other interesting varieties no longer available in Great Britain can be obtained. The varieties in the available field have been examined in some detail and show good and less good features; the latter covers the incidence of diseases, which are mentioned on page 132 and will be referred to again later. In the meantime, however, I would like to recall the statement (page 17) that the available field (excluding climbers) in Britain has dropped in a period of ten years from 390 varieties to 261, and of the latter well over seventy can be obtained from only one nurseryman (not necessarily the same one). At the time in question I was discussing with Jack Harkness – a 'comparative' (1962) newcomer to hybridising – his Yesterday (page 91) and his new hybrid tea Alexander. Our correspondence produced from him:

> No, I am not at all confident that Alexander will survive where Super Star fell, the life of a Hybrid Tea or Floribunda appears to be short indeed. We are breeding replacements and I fear it is in the nature of things for the lives of them to become progressively shorter. The outlook would be pessimistic without the belief that the *genus rosa* has the stuff in it somewhere to yield more beauty than we have yet seen. Whether that beauty is what the customer wants is another matter, inviting quite a vista of speculation on man's place in the world and his relationship to truth. Anyhow I have no heart to breed temporary replacements, and am putting my eggs in a more fragile basket, and hang the finance.
>
> Just you watch, I'll find gorgeous hybrid teas, by the dozen, now that I am not trying.

Jack Harkness is to my surprise fifty-five years old but, not to my surprise, he is described by his wife as a craftsman and not a business man.

I considered, indeed I felt a need to make a factual examination of the statement above: 'We are breeding replacements ... in the nature of things for the lives of them to be progressively shorter.' Here I interpose for the information of readers who do not see the literature of the Royal National Rose Society that, among other publications, it makes available from time to time *Roses – A Selected List of Varieties* under various headings. Here and later on, I shall confine myself for simplicity's sake to the hybrid teas and floribundas because these are the sorts which gardeners, public parks and so on in the British Isles buy the most – almost 35 million each year. That figure compares on my estimate of under 300,000 wild and old garden roses. But as regards the latter, one should mention that they have survived for any number of years up to, may we say, 100?

The *Selected List* has been compiled as a guide to the amateur rose grower: it gives the essential information about the varieties in the various classes of roses and no less than twenty-six special selections for particular purposes from the general list. The primary basis of selection is that the individual variety should be obtainable from at least five rose nurserymen. As already indicated, we shall confine ourselves to the hybrid teas and floribundas. Here I use those dated 1964 and 1971 (the latest) and jump over, for the sake of simplicity, that of 1967 and make the following comparison:

NUMBER OF VARIETIES OF HYBRID TEAS AND FLORIBUNDAS AVAILABLE

	1964	1971
Hybrid Teas	186	153
Floribundas	140	134
	326	287

NUMBER OF VARIETIES IN THE 1964 SELECTED LIST NOT APPEARING IN THAT OF 1971

		Percentage of 1964
Hybrid Teas	99	53%
Floribundas	92	65%
	191	58%

Put another way: out of 326 varieties of hybrid teas and floribundas available in 1964 in the commercial market, which is perhaps a measure of popular choice and demand – *vox populi, vox Dei* – only 135 had survived into 1971. That number having been augmented by 152 new arrivals to give the 1971 total of 287, made up of 153 hybrid teas and 134 floribundas.

I do not regard it as within the province of an amateur writer about wild and old garden roses to comment on figures of this kind except to suggest that they do seem to confirm the extracts from my correspondence with Jack Harkness. There is, however, another aspect – the incidence in the ordinary gardens, of the great majority containing some roses and therefore rose diseases. Here I fully realise, one touches on a sensitive subject, but one which ought to be brought out into the open if the evolution of the *genus rosa* is to continue its premier place in the horticultural world.

It has been noted earlier that the wild species roses do not appear to suffer much, if at all, from diseases.

If we look again at that 1971 edition of the *Selected List of Varieties* we will find that the Society included in some cases warnings about the susceptibility of a variety to diseases or, occasionally, to the effects of rain. This began in a modest way in the 1964 edition, but here one is not concerned with making comparisons. The statements in 1971 provide a sufficient illustration and show:

VARIETIES WITH WARNINGS
ABOUT LIABILITY TO DISEASES

	Hybrid Teas	Floribundas
Black spot	23	9
Mildew	19	7
Rust	1	1
'Disease'	5	6
	—	—
	48	23
	71	
Percentage of 1971 totals	31%	17%
	287	
Percentage of combined totals	24%	

So much for what the *Selected List* shows us on, one might term, the negative view. Perhaps, however, we ought to comfort ourselves that on this information, of 153 varieties of hybrid teas, two-thirds do not suffer from rose diseases nor, in 134 floribundas, do seventeen out of twenty.

In the section of *A Selected List of Varieties* devoted to ' ... Old Garden Roses, Rose Species and Hybrids of Garden Value', which contains about 138 of the varieties dealt with in this book, only four have a warning about diseases – all black spot.

Additionally the Society provides other confirmation – about the incidence of disease. Each year it publishes in the *Rose Annual* 'The Rose Analysis', which makes audit ratings of rose varieties under various and most useful headings in relation to their performance in the previous summer. Here we shall be interested in those dealing with 'Hybrid Tea Roses for General Garden Cultivation – varieties introduced in the British Isles before 1968'; and the floribundas within the same period.

Assessment is made by the votes of expert amateurs and rose nurserymen, some sixty-one in all, and both tables include twenty-four varieties obtaining the highest number of points. As regards the table relating to the best twenty-four hybrid teas in the summer of 1973, I find it somewhat staggering – and I mean just that – in the *Selected List* dated 1971 that no less than six of them carry a warning of liability to disease, and two others have a warning 'impatient of rain'. To this one has to add that, of the varieties concerned, five were awarded the Society's Gold Medal and two the Certificate of Merit on their performance at the Trial Ground.

The corresponding table relating to floribundas gives seven disease warnings and of those six are Gold Medallists.

In *Roses for Enjoyment* a broad outline was given of the way in which the trials of new varieties are carried out at St Albans, where new varieties are judged on their performance during three growing seasons.

Throughout the three-year period, the plants will be observed each week during the summer by members of an expert committee of amateur and professional rose growers. If, on its performance, the committee considers that the variety should do reasonably well – proper cultivation being understood – in most gardens, then a Trial Ground Certificate is awarded.

In making judgement the following qualities are taken into account:

Vigour of growth; habit of growth; freedom from disease; beauty of form and/or garden value; colour; freedom and continuity of flowering; fragrance and general effect.

In addition the society awards its Gold Medal or Certificate of Merit. The Gold Medal is for varieties which in addition to satisfying the conditions for the Trial Ground Certificate 'have some novel or outstanding quality or supersede a similar variety which has declined'. As one may infer, the Certificate of Merit is for the varieties which do not quite make the Gold Medal grade. Then there is the Edland Memorial Medal, awarded each year for the most fragrant rose that gained a Trial Ground Certificate or better.

The standards of the New Seedling Judging Committee are high, very high, and they should be so. In the ten years 1963–72 just under 2,750 new varieties were sent to the Trial Ground by 44 raisers; 223 of them were considered worthy of an award – about one in thirteen. They were made up as to 15 Gold Medals, 70 Certificates of Merit and 138 Trial Ground Certificates.

It may also be of interest to know something about those candidates which did so very badly that they had to be removed before the end of their three-year period.

In the autumn of 1970, 319 new varieties were received for trial. When at the end of 1973 this '1970 entry' was due for removal only 100 remained: 219 having already been taken out on account of obvious inferiority or on account of susceptibility to disease. The latter cause I believe accounted for 90 per cent of the 219. This '1970 entry', 319, at the end of the day had gained thirteen Trial Ground Certificates and three Certificates of Merit: no Gold Medals were awarded. In the successful sixteen there were – two hybrid teas, ten floribundas, two climbers and one miniature rose. It may be that this '1970' entry was untypical and/or unlucky in the growing weather of its three seasons: the percentage of awards to entries was 5 per cent, while that for the ten-year period, 1963–72, was 8 per cent.

Be this comparison what it may, no one could accuse the Society of adopting low standards – nor indeed of applying ones which are too high, having regard to its responsibilities to the membership and to gardeners generally, who buy 35 million rose plants each year.

It would seem that we are prepared to go on accepting the present incidence of rose diseases and the relative short life of the modern hybrid teas and to a lesser extent of the floribundas. In short: is our attitude one of acquiescence to a situation in which the many people who want roses in their garden must pay not only for the roses, but must also lavish much time and money in spraying them too? And should we accept, as being quite in the ordinary course, statements such as:

... it became very susceptible to rust disease (1954)

... developed a susceptibility to mildew (1956)

... its only fault is an unfortunate liability to black spot (1959)

... has been displaying an increasing tendency to contract mildew and, in some districts, black spot too (1960)

... appears to be reasonably resistant to disease except in areas where rust is prevalent (1961)

... there is a moderate susceptibility to black spot (1963)

... susceptible to black spot and, to a lesser degree, mildew (1964)

... On the debit side ... may take black spot, though less quickly than most roses in my garden (1965)

... the foliage ... has so far proved to be above average health in my own garden (1967)

These nine comments relating to nine different varieties have been taken from those made in an article in the 1973 *Rose Annual* about the nineteen winning varieties, between 1952 and 1971, of the President's International Trophy, which is awarded to the most outstanding Gold Medal Rose (if any) in each particular year. The year of award to the variety concerned is noted in each case. (No award was made in 1962, nor in 1966.)

Personally, I have been prepared to pay the price, but I wonder whether my increasing admiration for the wild and to a lesser extent the old garden roses owes something to a feeling that I do not wish to pay it much longer. It looks, however, that on sale figures I am one of a very small minority.

Nevertheless I would like to end this chapter in something of the same way in which it was begun. But first may I repeat what Sam McGredy said in a letter to me in 1972 and is recorded in *Roses for Enjoyment*, page 47: 'Incidentally the older I get, the more I realise that you cannot really tell what a rose is like until thousands of people have grown it ... It is only then that the variety will really show its true worth.'

This seems so very apposite in relation to the quotations on this page about how the President's Trophy winners are turning out.

But to continue on the theme which the thoughts of Jack Harkness (page 135) instigated in me. It was to get Sam McGredy's reactions to them. What follows is my edition of a taped reply in Northern Irish–New Zealand English as transcribed by an English-speaking German audio-typist!

139

You would like to know my reaction to a statement: 'The life of a hybrid tea or floribunda appears to be very short indeed. We, the hybridists, are breeding replacements in the theory that in the nature of things their lives have become progressively shorter. The outlook would be pessimistic without the belief that the *genus rosa* has in it somewhere the stuff to yield more beauty than we have yet seen.'

Well, I will go along with that: the reason I think that the life of a rose is becoming shorter is that competition is much more intense. There are a lot more people hybridising than before and as we breed more and more roses the 'collapses' show up more quickly and more prominently. But I don't think that is so, relatively. Just now one might think so, because all of a sudden Piccadilly, Peace, Super Star and several other very famous roses seem to be going down at the same time, but I think that this may be just chance. Another reason is that because of plant patents (and therefore the increase in the price of the varieties concerned) fewer nurserymen are inclined to take up new roses: this means that if they start off in twenty catalogues instead of a hundred, the chance of them dropping out of that twenty appears much more than if they were among a hundred. Even so, there will always be ten or twelve out of the hundred who will continue to grow a variety long after the raisers' dream has dissolved. I am thinking now over what the old days were like, when for example, McGredy's Sunset and McGredy's Yellow had ceased to be generally grown, but one could still find nurserymen in the country who had them. [Today six offer Sunset and seventeen the Yellow.]

'The outlook would be pessimistic now.' I do not think the outlook is pessimistic at all. Look, for example, at my own stuff currently in the Trial Ground and note the progressions I am getting out of what originally was a *R. spinosissima* shrub – Frühlingsmorgen × Orange Sweetheart crossed with Marlene × Evelyn Fison, to produce Picasso. You will see that there is a lot of new blood and a lot of new life there. I think too, of Reimer Kordes' beautiful hybrid tea seedlings with bright red on the edge of each lavender petal. I thought these were most attractive. So in the present stream of breeding there are, or will be, new things coming out. Yet I thoroughly agree with the sentiment that we have not started yet. As you say, very few of the wild species of the *genus rosa* have been brought into the make up of our popular modern hybrids. I am too old to start with new wild species seedlings. I will continue with Frühlingsmorgen and *R. microphylla coryana*. When one sees a bed of ground cover plants, including for example, Max Graf [page 56], Lady Curzon [page 56], *R. paulii* and *R. paulii rosea* [page 57], and look, for example, at Temple Bells now in the Trial Ground, you will see why I think there is an enormous future in this kind of rose. *R. davidii* I think worth using and *R. sweginzowii* and *R. polliniana*. It is possible to bring in species which will breed roses with fragrant foliage. I think *R. setipoda* is worth using – there are dozens of them. But as I have said: I am too old and it has got to be someone lucky enough to begin where I began, that is at age twenty, who is going to make the grade and that sort of thing.

As to 'even more beauty': I have a strong feeling that the rose as a plant is one of the ugliest shrubs in the garden today. When it is in flower it is very nice, but the method of pruning, particularly, is such that one tends to leave a long stalk and to get the new growth on top leaving the plant bare lower down. Now, for a lot of the whole rose year the rose foliage is either mildewed, black spotted or generally ugly. I am comparing it with say, in this country [New Zealand], the hibiscus where one has a beautiful plant for twelve months of the year, even when it is not in flower. With roses, for a lot of the year there is absolutely nothing there. Foliage has gone if one has pruned vigorously or young foliage, sitting on the top of bare stalks, does not look very pretty. Of course if one prunes right down to ground level there is some improvement, but then the quantity of flowers is much reduced.

So let us start again at the very beginning, with the proposition that – it will be very nice to raise a plant with rose flowers.

Now, if one is young enough the next question will be – what do we mean by a plant? Well, I think a plant which sticks straight up in the air is not very graceful; something that arches to the ground or else is densely covered with foliage from top to bottom, giving a true shrubby effect, is better. I think to get the densely foliaged plant with many shoots covered with flowers from top to bottom would be a very tall order. It could be done, I suppose, but it would be much more difficult then to have a plant which arched gracefully to the ground, it is true that many of the wild species do that to some extent already. It would be difficult, but I do not see really why it cannot be done. One should also think in terms of the foliage being fragrant. There is absolutely no reason why we cannot have roses with fragrant foliage giving perfume all the year round, whether they have flowered or not. One could also think in terms of foliage persisting for twelve months in the year. Look, for example, at Pink Favourite which even in the UK can almost achieve that period, as do some of the Wichuraiana ramblers. When, however, you chase after all these kind of things, the classic hybrid tea kind of bloom – which the amateur demands – would to a very large extent, disappear. One might have to be content with having in mind the kind of rose which first of all is in single or semi-double form and then, perhaps, a rather flat centred flower like so many of the old garden roses. But I do not know: fifty years from now, a hundred years from now, it should be possible to have what I have tried to envisage, at least in floribunda-like clusters on a charming plant.

So that is where I would like to see the rose going if I were starting again at age twenty, but I am too old and the pressures on a commercial rose breeder are so enormous to churn out something (to use an expression) that will return money. They are so great that I question if they will really allow the time to be given to such an object. If I could live long enough I would probably have a better chance here because hybridising costs are about one third of what they were in the UK and I have enough commercial varieties already to keep me going for the next ten years – so I could make a start on a new line, but what is the point? Who is going to finish it?

Now your second question: 'How are you getting along with your idea of breaking new ground with the use of unused species? And has there been anything done about the old garden roses?'

I am getting on to a certain extent. You can see the results in Picasso; brighter colours and interesting plant types, but it is, in terms of progress, no more than having produced an amoeba compared with a whale – indeed, a very small drop in the ocean – tiny, tiny improvement. I do not think there have been really any enormous improvements from the use of the wild species in my time. It takes donkeys years, or do I mean a whale of a time?

I have not used old garden roses because I do not think that is really the way to go. It is only rehashing what has been done from the time of Empress Josephine [page 22]. The real chance of improvement is going to come by going back to one of the original wild species.

I add one final extract from this tape: if only to illustrate once again what was described in *Roses for Enjoyment* about the work and the size of the operations which are involved in commercial hybridisation:

As a matter of interest a 120ft × 30ft glasshouse with about 200 rose plants in it produced 15,000 crosses, 10,000 seed pods (heps) – they yielded about 8lb of seed – quite a small box – and evoked: 'My God, all that work, sweat and what have you, and that is the end result.' But, of course, that 8lb of seeds will give me up to 100,000 seedlings. It could be worth a million dollars! You just really do not know.

Jack Harkness agrees with all that Sam McGredy has said, except in one particular – the question of age. After all, a man of fifty-five years is not so terribly ancient and, he says, 'to take only two steps towards the distant goal would be better than to die without having taken one'.

It is not within the author's province as an ordinary gardener, nor within his ability, to add anything to what has been said in this chapter.

But perhaps, however, I might allow myself to bring to the notice of the rose hybridists what Alice was told by the Red Queen – 'you're in the Second Square to begin with: in the Eighth Square ... we shall be Queens together, and it's all feasting and fun!'

I do think, however, that it is within the province of an ordinary, albeit an aged, gardener but a young admirer of the rose, to point again to the statistical story with which this chapter begins. There are, however, many stories about the incidence of diseases, the efficiency of the preventative nostrums, the effective lives of the modern rose varieties. In 1976 the Royal National Rose Society will be looking back, with conventional celebrations and speeches, on its then first 100 years and looking forward to the future. Might one suggest, as a modest beginning, that the Society embark on a really professional, objective and factual survey among its 100,000 members and affiliated societies, directed to finding out just what is the incidence of the diseases which afflict our modern roses and the old ones too, what remedies seem best and under what conditions?

I am afraid that such an enterprise will cost the Society rather more than the 1 per cent of its yearly income with which, at present, it subsidises academical research touching on these matters.

My second suggestion is that, following the practice of the senior society, the Royal Horticultural Society in having groups, for example, the Lily Group, the Society should consider forming a Wild and Old Garden Roses Group.

It seems auspicious that the Society's Hon Scientific Adviser and a great lover of the wild and old roses – E. F. Allen – is now occupying the premier position of President. In the meantime we ordinary gardeners can only work for the preservation and conservation of the old garden roses and hope for the rehabilitation of the wild roses in the future. For my part, I echo the words of Lady Denville in Georgette Heyer's *False Colours*: 'Exactly so! I cannot think how I endured those commonplace roses for so long.'

GLOSSARY

Mrs Gore said that her *Rose Fancier's Manual* had been 'put together for the use of the inexperienced English amateur: and, in order to make it practically available, scientific terms have been as far as possible laid aside, and the simplest form of language adopted'.

The author of this present book has had something of the same aim, but in case, like Mrs Gore, he has not been completely successful, the following may help to assuage it.

Visible flower structure: working upwards from the tip of the stalk, one begins with the *receptacle* carrying a circle of *sepals*, which are small greenish leaves, usually touching each other at the base, and together they form the *calyx*.

Then come the *petals* (see below): which incidentally form together a landing platform for insects.

Within that circle are first the *stamens*, each of these consists of a fine stalk carrying the *anther* which produces the *pollen*.

In the centre of the stamens, and therefore of the flower, and at a higher level are a number of *carpels* each carrying at the tip the *stigma*, through which the pollen (either from the flower's own anther or that brought in by insects) reaches and fertilises the ovule within the carpel. Usually the carpels are not separated and standing free but are united to form what is called the *pistil* (an old term for which is pointel) and the seeds within form the ovary.

In due course a flower dies: if it has been fertilised the sepals, petals and stamens normally fall off and the ovary develops into a fruit, which in the case of the rose is called a *hep*. They are of all shapes and sizes and may carry the dried sepals, stamens on the rim. Some may be covered in moss, eg, *R. centifolia muscosa* and *R. c. cristata*.

Blooms: petals or, if preferred, Petallage, enter into descriptions of roses: the definitions adopted by the Royal National Rose Society are – Double: those normally having more than twenty petals; Semi-Double: those having between eight and twenty; Single: those having less than eight.

144

In the case of some flattish, very double, old roses with short petals, those tightly packed in the centre fold over into the receptacle. Unable to open they result in a – **Button or Button Eye**. The description is apt as it really does resemble a green button without threadholes. An example can be seen in Königen von Dänemark on page 70 and in Cardinal de Richelieu on page 65.

Shape: *flat or sliced-off* are best described by looking at Fantin-Latour on page 52; *cup-shaped* are fairly obvious but illustrated are Cardinal de Richelieu, page 34, Alain Blanchard, page 63, and Louise Odier, page 52; *globular* is rather obvious, for readers who are doubtful can look at Raubritter, page 38; *pompon*: the blooms are the shape of those things that appear on the conical hats of pierrots; *quartered*: describe petals of a bloom, although regularly arranged, nevertheless form themselves into four sections or quarters. Examples are Reine des Violettes, page 86

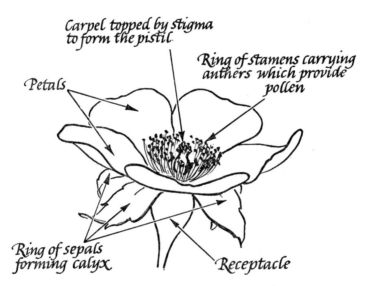

and Empereur du Maroc, page 86; *quilled*: refers to petals tubular in shape, those of the daisy have been offered as an example, but the cactus dahlia is much better.

Incidentally, the gallica Du Maître d'École exhibits flatness, quartering and a button eye, absence of illustration is regretted.

Green eye: it refers to the bud of a new shoot which comes in between a stem and a leaf stalk – when suitable for propagation purposes it is called a 'budding eye'.

Hybrid: 'a plant obtained by the pollen of one species on the stigma of another'. As regards roses one can use the word 'variety' as an alternative to 'species'.

Parentage: is the names of the two species or varieties so used. That of the seed parent (ie, the stigma) is given first and the provider of the pollen second, eg, Blanche Moreau (Comtesse de Murinais × Quatre Saisons Blanc Mousseux).

Pegging down: consists in fixing the stems, as shown in the illustration, right on the ground as one would with Max Graf, *R. wichuraiana*, its progeny and other ground coverers. The expression also refers to pegging down the tips only of long growing shoots, from old garden varieties so as to enhance their arching and to induce flowering shoots along them – suitable subjects for this treatment are suggested in Appendix A.

Sport: is a colloquial expression for a mutation, which is a change or alteration resulting in the production of a new species or variety. Actually Mrs Gore's definition cannot be bettered, it is 'flower [understood] or branch losing the habit of the plant on which it grows and assuming new specific characters'. The change of character can be progressive or sudden, and may relate to only a part of a plant. In such cases the changes can be preserved by grafting or budding the changed feature on to a root stock: thus setting up a new variety.

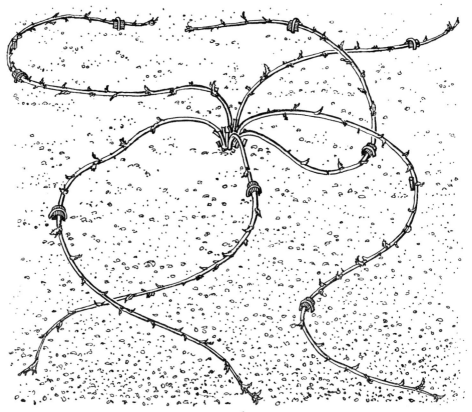

Pegging down

Spur pruning: consists in cutting a short branch, on which flowers (or fruit) have been borne, to two or three eyes (ie, buds).

Sucker: does not refer to one of those people said to be born every minute, but to a shoot arising from below ground: such a definition might be held to cover the lateral increase, as for instance that of *R. spinosissima* described on page 28 and all other roses grown on their *own roots*. In practice it refers particularly to roses grown on stocks, eg, *canina*, and is a shoot sent up from that stock and not one from the rose variety – left alone it may take over, submerge and destroy the latter.

APPENDIX A

SUMMARIES OF VARIETIES WITH SIMILAR CHARACTERISTICS

The number following the name is that of the page on which the variety is described.

Recurrent bloom
In addition to the Bourbons and Hybrid Perpetuals (Chapter 9) and the Chinas (Chapter 9):
Blanche Moreau (80)
Comte de Chambord (75)
Deuil de Paul Fontaine (84)
fedtschenkoana (49)
Frühlingsmorgen (31)
Jacques Cartier (75)
Mme de la Roche-Lambert (87)
Mousseline (81)
Pink Grootendorst (56)
Quatre Saisons (71)
Rugosas (53–5)
Salet (84)
Sarah van Fleet (57)
Schneezwerg (57)
Stanwell Perpetual (29)
Climbers:
Alister Stella Gray (121)
Amadis (111)
Blush Noisette (119)
bracteata (113)
Celine Forestier (120)
Desprez à fleur jaune (120)
Gloire de Dijon (120)
Mme Alfred Carrière (121)
Maréchal Niel (120)
Mermaid (113)

moschata (116)
Sombreuil (115)

Old garden roses with lax growth (*see* page 127)
In addition to those marked * below:
Blairii No 2 (97)
Blanche Moreau (80)
Jeanne de Montfort (81)
Mme Ernst Calvat (96)
Mme Isaac Periere (96)
Tour de Malakoff (78)
William Lobb (82)

Scramblers and ground coverers (*see* page 127)
Félicité et Perpétue (122)
Lady Curzon (56)
macrantha (37)
Mme Plantier (70)
Max Graf (56)
†*paulii* (56)
†*p. rosea* (57)
†*wichuraiana* and its ramblers (122–3)

Need pegging down (*see* p 147)
In addition to those marked † above:
Baron Giraud de l'Ain (106)
centifolia muscosa (Common Moss) (80)
Frau Karl Druschki (106)

Gruss an Teplitz (98)
Honorine de Brabant (98)
Hugh Dickson (107)
La Reine Victoria (94)
Mme Ernst Calvat (96)
Mme Pierre Oger (94)
Paul Neyron (101)
Reine des Violettes (96)

Blooms with lilac, purple and maroon colours

Belle de Crécy (64)
Capitaine John Ingram (82)
Cardinal de Richelieu (65)
Charles de Mills (65)
Deuil de Paul Fontaine (84)
Du Maître d'Ecole (67)
Gloire de Ducher (101)
Hippolyte (67)
President de Sèze (66)
Prince Charles (96)
Reine des Violettes (96)
Robert le Diable (78)
Souvenir d'Alphonse Lavallée (100)
Souvenir du Dr Jamain (101)
Tour de Malakoff (78)
Tuscany (64)
Tuscany Superb (64)
Veilchenblau (118)
Violette (119)
William Lobb (82)

Striped and Parti-coloured Blooms

Baron Giraud de l'Ain (106)
Camaieux (66)
Commandant Beaurepaire (98)
Ferdinand Pichard (98)
Honorine de Brabant (98)
Perle des Panachées (67)
Roger Lambelin (105)
Rosa Mundi (63)
Tricolore de Flandre (67)
Variegata (78)
Variegata di Bologna (98)
Vicks Caprice (106)

Heps of Quality and/or Quantity

alba semiplena (69)
altaica (28)
atropurpurea (53)
canina andersonii (32)
filipes (113)
forrestiana (44)
Frau Dagmar Hastrup (54)
helenae (115)
highdownensis (46)
longicuspis (113)
macrantha (37)
macrophylla (47)
micrugosa (58)
moyesii (45)
moyesii Geranium (45)
moyesii Sealing Wax (45)
multibracteata (48)
Rambling Rector (118)
rubiginosa (38)
rubrifolia (41)
rugosa alba (53)
Scabrosa (54)
setipoda (48)
soulieana (44)
spinosissima (28)
sweginzowii (43)
virginiana (40)
webbiana (42)
willmottiae (44)
woodsii-fendleri (27)

Foliage

(a) *Grey-Green*
dupontii (123)
fedtschenkoana (49)
Frühlingsmorgen (31)
hibernica (35)
multibracteata (48)
pomifera duplex (42)
rubrifolia (41)
soulieana (44)
spinosissima et al (28)
(b) *Ferny, Lacey or Dainty*
californica plena (27)
Canary Bird (26)
cantabrigiensis (26)

farreri persetosa (43)
highdownensis (46)
moyesii (45)
moyesii Geranium (45)
moyesii Sealing Wax (45)
spinosissima et al (28)
sweginzowii (43)
webbiana (42)
willmottiae (44)
woodsii fendleri (27)
(c) *Fragrant*
primula (27)
rubiginosa (38)
setipoda (48)

Generally thornless stems
Amadis (111)
banksiae (112)
dupontii (123)
*Kathleen Harrop (95)
Lykkefund (115)
Mme de Sancy de Parabère (112)
*Mme Legras de St Germain (70)
*Mme Plantier (70)
Morlettii (112)
Mrs John Laing (102)
Prince Charles (96)
Violette (119)
*Zéphirine Drouhin (97)

APPENDIX B

WHERE TO SEE WILD AND OLD ROSES

It has seemed to the author to be somewhat inadequate to write a book about wild and old garden roses without offering to those readers whose land interest may have been roused in relation to their own gardens, *in esse* or *in posse*, where those roses may be seen, criticised, appraised and judged.

This appendix includes gardens of various kinds where wild and/or old garden roses can be seen, the owners and where further particulars may be sought. But pray remember that even though the object of your visit may be disappointing, there could well be recompense in the other plants, trees, flowers and so on that may be seen.

The gardens have been included on the basis of information kindly made available to the publishers and this whole appendix could not have been completed without the kind co-operation of Ms Lily Shohan and the Brooklyn and New York Botanical Garden.

Arnold Arboretum of Harvard University, Jamaica Plain, Massachusetts 02130
Balboa Park, San Diego, California 92101
Birmingham Botanical Garden, 2612 Lane Park Road, Birmingham, Alabama 35223
Bishop's Garden, Washington Cathedral, Washington, DC 20016
Brooklyn Botanical Garden, 1000 Washington Avenue, Brooklyn, NY 11225
Descanso Gardens, 1418 Descanso Drive, La Canada, California 91011
Edisto Gardens, US 301 South, Orangeburg, South Carolina 29115
Elizabeth Park Rose Garden, Prospect and Asylum Avenues, Hartford, Connecticut 06103
Fort Worth Botanical Garden Center, 3220 Botanical Garden Drive, Fort Worth, Texas 76107
Hershey Rose Gardens and Arboretum, Hershey, Pennsylvania 17033
Hodges Gardens, Box 921, Many, Louisiana 71449
Karl Jones, Barrington, Rhode Island 02806
Joseph J. Kern Rose Nursery, Box 33, Mentor, Ohio 44060

Memphis Botanical Garden, Audobon Park, 750 Cherry Road, Memphis, Tennessee 38117

Missouri Botanical Garden, 2315 Tower Grove Avenue, St Louis, Missouri 63110

Norfolk Botanical Gardens, Airport Road, Norfolk, Virginia 23518

Peidmont Park, Peidmont Road, Atlanta, Georgia 30309

Queens Botanical Garden Society, 43–50 Main Street, Flushing, New York 11355

Reynolds Gardens, Wake Forest University, Box 7325 Reynolda Station, Winston-Salem, North Carolina 27109

Rose Hill Memorial Park, 3900 Worloman Mill Road, Whittier, California 90601

Sarah P. Duke Garden, Duke University, Durham, North Carolina 27706

Thomasville Nurseries, Inc, PO Box 7, Thomasville, Georgia 31792

Richard Thomson, 415 Wister Road, Wynnewood, Pennsylvania 19096 (please call before visiting 212-MI-22305)

Tyler Rose Garden Center, Tyler Rose Park, Box 2039, Tyler, Texas 75701

BIBLIOGRAPHY

Bunyard, Edward A. *Old Garden Roses* (1936)
Berrisford, Judith. *The Wild Garden* (1966)
Cecil, David. *Lord M.* (1954)
Dickens, Charles. *Pickwick Papers* (1836–7)
Edwards, Gordon. *Roses for Enjoyment* (1962, 1973)
Gore, Mrs. *The Rose Fancier's Manual* (1838)
Hessayon, Dr D. G. and J. P. *The Garden Book of Europe* (1973)
Hillier & Sons. *Catalogue of Roses and Fruit* (1973–4)
Jekyll, Gertrude and Mawley, Edward. *Roses for English Gardens* (1966)
Kingsley, Rose G. *Roses and Rose Growing* (1908)
Le Grice, E. B. *Rose Growing Complete* (1965)
McClintock, David. *Companion to Flowers* (1966)
McGredy, S. and Jennett, S. *A Family of Roses* (1971)
Paul, W. *Roses and Rose Culture*; *The Rose Garden* (1848, 1872 et seq)
Paul & Son. *Catalogues* (1864–98)
Pemberton, Rev Joseph H. *Roses* (1908)
Rivers, Thomas. *The Rose Amateur's Guide* (1872)
Shepherd, Roy E. *History of the Rose* (1954)
Sidney, Samuel. *Rides on Railways* (1851, 1973)
Steen, Nancy. *The Charm of Old Roses* (1966)
Thomas, Graham S. *Old Shrub Roses* (1955)
   Shrub Roses of To-day (1962)
   Manual of Shrub Roses (1964)
   Climbing Roses Old and New (1965)
   – see also under Royal National Rose Society
Thomas, H. H. *The Rose Book* (1913)

Books of Reference:

The Concise Oxford Dictionary of Current English
A Dictionary of Botany, Usher, G.
Dictionary of National Biography (1890)
Dictionary of Roses, Gault, S. M. and Synge, P. M.
Encyclopaedia Britannica (1955)

A Glossary of Botanic Terms, Jackson, R. B.
Larousse, Grand, – Encyclopédique
Larousse – Illustre – Dictionnaire Encyclopédique
Modern Roses VI, McFarland, J. H.
Oxford Dictionary of Quotations
Pears Cyclopaedia
A Popular Dictionary of Botanical Names and Terms, Zimmer, G. F.
A Smaller Classical Dictionary, Blackeney, E. H.
Whitaker's Almanack

Royal National Rose Society (Editor Leonard Hollis); *A Selected List of Varieties*; *The Cultivation of the Rose*; *The Rose Annual*, articles in the years indicated, by –

Aldous, Hobel M. (1965)
Allen, Tess (1968, 1970, 1971, 1972, 1973)
Borchard, Ruth (1966)
Gault, S. M. (1972)
Lindsay, Nancy (1957)
Mayer, Theo (1970)
Mead, Daisy L. (1955)
Morrison, Barbara (1968)
Thomas, G. S. (1951, 1953, 1954, 1958, 1962, 1964, 1965, 1966, 1967, 1969, 1973)
Witchell, F. C. H. (1973)

'A man will turn over half a library to make one book': so said Dr Johnson (1709–84) and with prescience too, because he was followed by Martin Joseph Routh (1755–1854) with his – 'You will find it is a very good thing to verify your references, Sir!'

INDEX

Numbers in **bold type** refer to main references, those in *italic* indicate plate pages